EL~SHABAZZ

99 ATTRIBUTES OF A POEM

"I have written only one poem from different angles..." El~Shabazz

EL~SHABAZZ

99 ATTRIBUTES

99 ATTRIBUTES OF A POEM

Copyright © 2015 **Kimathi El~Shabazz**

All rights reserved. No part of this book may be reproduced or transmitted in any form or by any means, electronic or mechanical, including photocopying, recording, or by any information storage and retrieval system, without permission in writing from the publisher. All questions and/or request are to be submitted to: 134 Andrew Drive, Reidsville NC, 27320.

To the best of said publisher's knowledge, this is an original manuscript and is the sole property of author **KIMATHI EL~SHABAZZ**

Printed in the United States of America

ISBN-13: 978-0692475898
ISBN-10: 0692475893

Printed by Createspace 2015
Published by BlaqRayn Publishing Plus 2015

99 ATTRIBUTES

Dedication To:

My Lord
My Mother,
My Family,
My People,
&
The Truth!!!

El~Shabazz

99 ATTRIBUTES

* The Old Woman Said #16 *

The Old Woman said We are two halves of a Whole,
But that Now-a-Days, Most Men are not Half the Man of a Woman and Most Women will have to learn to be Women again from the few Men who remember who they Once were....
She said we are too Cheap in our Thoughts and spend far too much in looking less than our Worth...
She said our mirrors laugh at us like the Mockery of Children who Shatter our False image,
like I don't know where that Child get that from, not only does the Apple not fall far from the Tree, its of the same Seed....
She said the trouble with Love is y'all ain't got no Training, Love is taught like any Skill... And Mothers who use to Master the Craft have become Charlatans of their own Trade calling it Man-Made,...
She said you Fathers have robbed your Daughters and cheated your Sons and they will remember your thievery and charge you with the embezzlement of their souls and bring you to the Judgment Halls of Justice, Convict you before the World, Hang you in

99 ATTRIBUTES

the Public Square and Dare any Man to
Price his
Head...
She said our leaders are followers of their
lowest Desires, We couldn't ask for Less
with so much on the
Line , how much Naked Truth can they hide
as they Parade Flamboyantly down Main
Street in Well Dressed
Lies...
She said Lovers Lane is full of Dead Ends
and Muggings, Kissing and Hugging under
Street Lamps could get you
Shot, Robbed and Beat Up... This ain't no
way to Treat Us and to Think , y'all had the
Best Examples in
Muhammad
And
Jesus...
The Old Woman said,.. Son you just keep
writing that Poetry or whatever they call it,
because there are no more Prophets and this
World doesn't Profit, all we have left are you
Few Raggedy Poets
and
You Remind me of a Smile I use to wear as
a Young Girl, come have a sip with me and
let me tell you where they hide the
Prettiest
Pearls...

99 ATTRIBUTES

* Lovers & Poets*

I whispered to my lover behind the veiled
kiss of a thousand lips,
I have so much to say and so few words, that
I have had to learn the language of birds,
just to say something as simple as this...

Just to watch the Sun set our table for two
on the balcony of intoxicated dreams and
red wine sillies that giggle us happy,
It was a curious case of confiscated dawns
held up to our lips, like a kiss between day
and night and she answered a question in me,
she never
asked me...

We have our love reasons that defy common
sense and we barter with our contradictions,
trying to find the best deal to kill time and
pocket the most from these stolen moments,
We were careful enough to get caught by the
Sunrise after a lazy lunar night of lunatic
love and lavish laughter , luxurious
linguistics found in the love lost
conversations of Lovers & Poets...

99 ATTRIBUTES

* Where Lovers Fall *

They say Love don't cost a thing, but ask the penniless broken hearts the price they paid for kisses that became homeless ..
We travel these fork roads, spooning with knives in our backs , broken dishes and stale wedding cake, it even made me a drunk for these sipping
Moments...

I tip my whine glass to the tears of tender souls who drown in their cries and gulp waterfalls of sadness ,
tear drop pond ripples sending crashing waves to the beach sand   footsteps of farewell
Lovers..
We turtleneck hickies and brisk cold loneliness , if cold hands make a warm heart, then frostbitten toes light the passion of poets under a frosted chilled moon cozy wrapped midnight
Cover...

We throw caution to the wind on the wings of lovebirds ,
we walk on kites and climb over skies, dive into our hearts dreams even when we should be alarmed
We press

99 ATTRIBUTES

Snooze...
We are blameless Lovers and daring fools, we walk by faith with our eyes wide shut, targets for daggers and betrayal , but cowards don't deserve Love and Love Soldiers are the first..Killed , Wounded and Bruised...

So I wear my heart on my sleeve in this shirtless love, craving her touch as she dip and lick her fingers of my chocolate skin yumminess , she chews me up,
Heart and All,...
I know the dangers of Love Battlefields and how defenseless I am on the frontline,
we war for love and I was shot in the Heart but never dropped my flag, so bury me in her Heart
Where
Lovers
Fall....

* As Pretty as She Is *

As pretty as she is, I've had just about enough of her cuteness , I mean we ain't gotta be ugly, but damn it, we're gonna sho' be Beautiful...

No lipstick or coverup , I got a naked truth that's knock knee and bashful and blushing roses with natural Shea butter honey nut gently laid over cinnamon stick collarbones and you ain't been this fresh since the midwives gave you your first bath and you burped your first laugh as smooth as spilled baby oil in a kitchen sink bubble bath, and not even dimples can stand a chance against your
Beautiful ....

As pretty as she is, she bet not twist her lips to say something cute,
I mean we ain't gotta be ugly , but damn it , we're gonna sho' be
Beautiful....

99 ATTRIBUTES

* Between Us *

It's not as easy as we pretend , if we don't leave with broken hearts, it'll damn Sho' take us for a
Bend,...
I mean we Pretty Tough but get Ugly in Weakness , Sleepless Attitudes can make for strange bed buddies , I mean She ain't said two words , talking like that all night, this conversation may never
End....

We hold our tongues because these words are razor sharp, we would hate to cut each other and slice through soul and bleed each other out,
If words hurt, then we got Murder in the Mouth...
This is Gut, Grit and Good God just get us to each others Lips, so we can say we made it by the Skin of our Kiss, our compromise got copper wire hanging out of it, trying to jump start and kick over this cold engine , so we can drive it Home,
I mean we just gotta
Work it
Out....

We swim Smiles through Tears and Swamp water Blues, we got enough blame to share

99 ATTRIBUTES

two plates at a Chinese Buffet, just to fill up
to feel empty... Got us asking did you
get
Enough.....
Don't
hold
this against me, but I'm Hard on Women,
because I'm so Soft in Love, every Cookie
Jar has its crumbs, She got her Baby Fat
stuck in my Love, She cries herself to sleep
while Sucking Thumb, and I ain't done til I
apologize for what she has done, because I
ain't got nothing to say for myself that she
hasn't accepted as that's
Just
Between
Us...

99 ATTRIBUTES

* It's So *

It's so unfair of you to stand in the view of my day,
To compromise my lightly clouded sky blue and undo the things I wanna
say...

It's so childish of you to spit pollaseeds in my dreams and leave this mess all over my smile,
Write my name on scratch paper with X's and O's, and crumble me up like a rough draft poem written on paper bag
brown,...

It's so pretty of you to paint your nails with my purple heart blush, daring me to snatch you by the hand and run off to where our legs can't
stand ,
I mean I didn't wanna put you on the spot and all, but you're so rude and clumsy to love me at a time like this, when I can't get you out of my head,
And you can't blame me for the things I've almost
said...

99 ATTRIBUTES

It's so like you to hush me up with
Beauty,
So now how can I talk about you and not sound
Looney...

99 ATTRIBUTES

* For Love *

Love ain't no cakewalk so take the icing off your toes,
This thang here is like walking on hot coals , it'll popcorn your toes,
So don't butter soft anything but your kisses, you gotta go hard like prison yard steel, chase water uphill, touch the inside of this thing you feel and ring it by the neck til it cough up its Heart and peel back these layers of Real...

You can't have roses without thorns, and yeah you're gonna prick yourself, like Ouch!!! You ungrateful Son of Adam, but his Momma had him , just for you, just for this moment, just for this lesson, rework your guessing, stop stressing and count your Blessings, light your moon, even if all you got is a
Crescent...

I know this Woman can get under your skin and become hard to reach like an itch at the upper center of your back, but damn ... How good it feels when you churn her to butter and watch her melt in your hands and she can't help but to puddle for a Real Man....

99 ATTRIBUTES

Ups and Downs, Smiles and Cries, Truths
and Lies, Hellos and Goodbyes and the late
coming answers to
Why...
The easy ain't worth it, and the hard will
make you wanna hurt it... It ain't pretty or
perfect , but if you know how to work it
with this person , you for certain , will dig
up treasures under measures of dirt, pain and
hurt like lifting up a curse and finding
hidden money in your wallet or
Purse ...

I'm'a kiss her on the back of the knee and
make her fall for me like waterfalls crashing
lips first   splashing over tongue ... Every
Spring we go Sprung... Every Summer we
go Simmer...,Every Fall we go
Awwww...and Every Winter I'm still
With Her...

99 ATTRIBUTES

* Morning Love Sickness *

I shouldn't have to write it on the Wall,
Hanging on Graffiti Bridge for the World
to see it All,
I Painted your Nails with it and Blushed you
like a Cherry Moon, we aren't just Lovers
Fukcin' off, in a bed full of melted Thighs,
and the floor full of Draws
And Bras,
We got Dreams too, Like Running off
into a Rain Cloud without umbrellas with
our mouths open like Wishing
Wells,
We Kiss and Tell, Like I Love You Too...
Ssshhhh, you shouldn't have to say The Too,
This is One Love, We don't got much Room,
We may have to share
One Cell,
We go Good Together like Lips and Kisses,
Pain and Prayers, Baby Fat and Wedding
Cake,
Thank God You Said You're Late,
I was looking at the Time like I couldn't
Wait, So I wrote it on a Wall,
That Morning Love Sickness is the
Only way to start your
Day....

99 ATTRIBUTES

* Looking @ Love *

We got this abstract love, pigeon toed and knock knee , got a silly walk to it, but just as cute as it can
Be...
We run our smiles into dimples and pinch a blush into this sweetness like sugar smacks all across our Cheeks...
She thinks I'm Him, and I think She's Her, and that's enough to convince us its a date with destiny and I was the perfect gentleman to let her get the
Best of Me...
I want to swing on her arm like a purse and slide down her hands like henna until she squeeze my charm in her palm, just my luck, she's into
Caressing Me...
Funny thing about these kind of kisses is they never dry out, its like kissing in the rain while chewing on Blow Pop Bubble Gum and drooling dreams into each others mouths and to think about her, I still can't get no
Sleep...
I just like to watch her stroll from the corner cafe through crowded clangorous conversations stepping over sounds with a gentle silence,

99 ATTRIBUTES

I like turning the volume down and watching her on an old Black and White TV...

99 ATTRIBUTES

* Aiming @ Poets *

They pushing Poets out of 7 story windows ,
for telling stories that don't add Up...
They stoning Poets for playing Prophet, with
no scriptures to back'um up, so carry their
cross and hang'um
Up...
They jailing Poets for stealing attention and
embezzling emotions under felonious
Fraud...
They socking Poets in the mouth for
mocking monks and making mention of
manuscripts that were mere memos and now
they gotta face a merciless
Mob...
They f*kcing Poets in the face for fondling
fantasies and freaking the font, being fancy
and frisky and faking at
Love....
They killing Poets for pimping the pen and
preaching it
phony,
impregnating the page and walking out on
the poem,
like you ain't paying for sh*t , but you
paying for this,
you can't pay it in panties and pennies...
You gotta pay it,
In
Blood....

99 ATTRIBUTES

And if they ain't aiming at Poets...
They aiming
At
Us!!!

99 ATTRIBUTES

* The Old Woman Said # 25 *

The Old Woman said, a Good Man is no match for a Bad Woman, as Tragic as The Ruins of a Good Woman snared by a Bad Man,
Heartbreak starts with kisses that shatter like tempered glass, it may feel Smooth but it has so many cracks in it,
it'll fall apart under a
Whisper...

As Beautiful as the Devil is, you think an Ugly Angel has a Chance at stealing your heart, so break all the mirrors in your eyes,
A Naked Truth and a Well Dressed Lie has confounded the Wise like Happy Fools Paradise...

The Old Woman said find you a crooked Woman with more Straight Lines than you, every Man needs a Woman as flawed as his Mother to find some correction in Himself...

Women are so close to God, they can act like devils
sometimes ,
for she knows that Man is but Clay in her hands, however you turn out, depends on the Woman who handled your

99 ATTRIBUTES

Soul....

The Old Woman said, Love your Women for you have no Power over them except that they give their Love to you,
You are entrusted with that which can Hurt you Most, like playing Persian Roulette with all 6 Bullets, there's just No Way Out of This,
So Kiss like your Life depends on it, her hand is ever on the Trigger, and for Love she'll turn the Gun on Herself,
She just can't live without Love and don't try to stop Her because She's no stranger to Blood,...

The Old Woman said, Son take these Jewels and give your Woman a Gift She can't Return...
Now let an Old Woman enjoy her drink before the
Earth turns...

99 ATTRIBUTES

* Ultimatums & Contradictions *

I can't let her go, but she can't stay here,
My heart can't run away and join the circus like hobo Love,
I'm walking the high wire rope and splitting hairs between my toes and She ain't strong enough to let
Go...
Too much the same with enough blame to have an equal share going in circles trying to be square, like this ain't fair... She must've put something in the
Air...
I can't breathe, I'm too close to her dreams and so far from her reality, if she was Solomon's concubine , he would've did something wise, but I'm too foolish to know what to do with it... Its so much easier to say you
Did
It....
If my Wife get scent of this like her nail polish , She'll put her finger on it and Say...' You Smell this Shit,
That ain't my perfume' ....
And collar lipstick is worse than hickies because now she knows the color of her Kisses...
I'm wishing I could catch my 22, like I dropped the ball 21 times, damned if I don't ,

99 ATTRIBUTES

damned if I do and now she wanna pull
away like she's the one with the
Ring...
Killing me with ultimatums like...
You ain't nothing to me...
Until...
You're
Everything...

99 ATTRIBUTES

* Unspoken *

Let us write a Poem together,
Then Sew us together at our Hips and Finger
Tips,
Let's forget what to Say, while Overdoing it,
Ruining a good conversation like what's
wrong with our
Lips,
I mean I can stop right here, and save the
rest for your Left Ear,
Run down a sequence of events, under the
secret of your scent that draws me
Near,
This is No Time for Words,
let's just undo our mouths,
And Unhook our Breath to get a Taste of the
Moment,
There's no better way to End a Poem, than a
Recital over the sand balconies of Cairo, and
Leave every Touch
Unspoken ...

99 ATTRIBUTES

* As Cute As She Is *

In the face of beautiful things, she can get pretty ugly
as cute as she is,...

The petals of a rose can cut steel under the sharpest pain, like I can sit still through this hurt,
as cute as she is...

Broken pieces of a heart can't hold a smile together even on a face like hers,
as cute as she is,...

Her touch feels colder breaking through the feathers of my goosebumps , she gotta chill with that,
as cute as she is...

The distance between a dimple and a smile can sadden any traveler who didn't bring a happy jug of water,
as cute as she is,...

Chapped lips of peeled back kisses can bleed at any moment just to speak her name,
as cute as she is...

99 ATTRIBUTES

Her secrets hide a whisper that can only be heard in her sleep, pillow talking can ruin any dream,
as cute as she is...

It'll kill me to stay for a love that's dead, and I plan to live to kiss another day, I dug myself into a hole, only to bury beautiful things,
As Cute As She Is...

99 ATTRIBUTES

* SILK & LINEN *

We got Hidden Histories and Stolen
Legacies,
A Treasure Chest of Buried Secrets in
Unmarked Graves and a String of
Ebonies,
Mahoganies, Keisha's and Khadijah's,
Ayana's and Tawana's and Our Favorite
Baby Momma's who Promise not to File
Child Support Papers,
If We Stop by Later...
With Greater Appreciation for
Amazing Grace,
The Best Attitude makes
The Prettiest Face,
Like Stretch Marks around the Waist
Is the Best Tasting
Cake,
And The Cookie Taste Great after a
Hot Plate,
Call us Prejudice, but we've Traveled the
World and The Seven Seas,
And Ain't No Women like the Women
Of Our
Race,
Ready, Set, Go... Even if She Trips and Fall,
Crack and Crawls , She still comes in
First Place,
Birthplace,... KUSH, all the way to the
Southern Bush, to the SunKissed

99 ATTRIBUTES

Women of YEMEN,
It's been a Minute,
Since I've Been in your Business
So Maybe we Should Carry this
conversation in your Belly,
And Continue Our History
In
SILK & LINEN ...

99 ATTRIBUTES

* Beautiful Reasons *

She was Beautiful for reasons unknown to herself,
I'm not talking pretty girl, I'm talking Lovely Woman, on the Bright Side of a Butterflied Moon,
Flung across a Smile so Gentle,
She splashed like Feathers into Clouds,
Woven into Quilted Skies and Cosmic Cushions Studded with Silver Star Emeralds,
Clustered in Cream Soda Milky Way Runoff and Sweet Twilight Drool,
With a Ruby Womb, Swirling Chocolate Waters,
The Primordial Honey Bean Soup and Organic Swim of our
Sons
and
Daughters,
She was Beautiful for all the right reasons and all the excuses
I needed for
Breathing ...

99 ATTRIBUTES

* Later Soon *

I was passing by the Sun
And Seen the Most Beautiful
Moon, under the Streetlights of
Afternoon,
Into the Traffic of Shooting
Stars and Crowded Stares
The Calls to Prayer were still
Fresh in the Air and Her Smile
Was like Silk in the
Loom,
It was a Melt Down in
Chocolate City, She made a
Beautiful thing so Pretty
Leaning against her Shadow
Giving me room to Ensued
I'm telling her things I should
Say Later
Soon...

99 ATTRIBUTES

* 9 Months & 7 Miles *

I want to seed your womb with passion fruit , root myself in your belly and see if you can stomach this love as it widens your nose and thickens your hair, with swollen feet because I made you plump with
Love..
Let's braid our love and grow inside you like pumpkin seeds I round you out like earth chronicles, past , present and future birth from a kiss that held the secret of life between our lips spoken between hips and legs that
Hug...
We broke love down into a single cell Adam , divided itself to multiple the building blocks of life's bloom with the sweetest waters splashing in your womb with Allah(swt) feeding The Soul with a spoon, you sleep with a
full belly resting your head on my
Smile ...
It's like you swallowed the Sun, Moon and Stars, This Universal Gift will stretch mark your skin to take breath and we blend it smooth with Shea Butter to Golden your Brown and saturate Our
Honey Child...
If I spill you life , will you spit me babies who burp the future and live our dreams,

99 ATTRIBUTES

recycle us through endless rebirth, I'll find you again over eons into the distant
Now...
I want to time travel in your womb under your liquid skies bask in your darkest lights into the phantoms of shape and form until you birth my cry and comfort me in your breast and arms, it's been
9 Months & 7 Miles...

99 ATTRIBUTES

* Wiped Away Kisses *

This dying Love is gasping for life,
Clinging to the breaking threads of our hearts,
Unraveling the yarn of our souls , as promises break,
Over our heads like empty wine bottles, toasting at a candle lit Dinner for two,
drinking our tears over entrees of Farewell, that are so hard to swallow,
Can I barrow your tomorrow , on a pinky promise ring I exchanged for these hearts of sorrow ,
Why did we break our wings and crash against rocks, break apart and spill our hearts so wastefully ,
If careless whispers, could shout and scream, it would echo the bells of your soul, and snap a rainbow,
These tears fall heaviest in rain as the earth weeps to share in our pain,
We balled up paper crushing hearts like scrap paper in yesterday's garbage cans ,
These discarded love notes
Are crumbled in my veins,
We use to reach back until we got use to the distance ,
these slamming doors and broken dishes,

99 ATTRIBUTES

Was when we still had passion, now we are silently violent , if truth hurts, silence kills, and We wiped away our Kisses...

99 ATTRIBUTES

Conscious Abstract

I'm the Prince of the Pen,
You Should King me
Now,
I got Concrete Roses and Silk Thorns in my
Crown with Faithful
Sins...

I got 12 Stellar Poems,
but One, I should crumble up now, or watch
it kiss my pen and betray
my Thoughts...
I'm a virgin birth, because Momma won't
say who
did it , She scribbled him out, now I gotta
Write that wrong, so I wrote these
Faults...

I rode an Ass through the City, She was half
way cute, 3 parts pretty, a Quarter Spoon
Crazy, but you should hear these Ladies...
Screaming Hallelujah and Crip-Walking in
The Street, but We're all One Blood, and
they're telling me to Preach my Poetry
Sermon and my Last Supper Belch, if you
steady your womb, you can carry my
Babies ...

Don't cry for me Nubia, it was written on my
birth certificate   , I would spill out my ink

99 ATTRIBUTES

and die on the paper , that's scripture, I'm
Psalms 72, believe me
That...
Hand me my Quran and a Cold Glass of
Truth, my childhood blanket won't cover my
naked, you can see write through me, like
holding paper up to the light, I cuddle
Lambs on World Corners,
I'm a Conscious
Abstract...

99 ATTRIBUTES

* The Old Woman Said # 26 *

The Old Woman said don't kiss on a full
belly, it'll give you heartburn,
If you bite your tongue, you'll bleed your
words, stop saving pain, spend it quickly,
better broke with a goofy smile than a wallet
full of sadness, poorly rich is 30 gold coins
and the price of betrayal ,
If you trust no man, you can't trust half of
yourself,
If you trust no woman ,you can't trust half of
yourself,
There is no other way for you to have gotten
here , you untrustworthy lump of
contradictions , how can you fix your mouth
against yourself with unsaid foolishness ,
As if you said the
Coolest
Shit,....

The Old Woman said, Woman is a Pussycat
with a Scorpions tail,
Careful how you stroke her,
Don't purr a pinch that pokes through your
pores and poach poison and pain , a pot of
passion is like hot grits,
It can warm your Belly or scold you in
Celsius,

99 ATTRIBUTES

So handle with Care and Share a slice of
Bean Pie with the one who's still there after
such an unfair day, it's relaxing to soak your
feet in a pair of hands that knows how to
unbraid stress like
Hair ...

The Old Woman said,
Man is an easy Happy, a Clumsy Comfort
and a Watchful Suspicion,
Provided Protector of Probabilities and
Possible Prophecies,
Precisely as He Projected, and He was Pretty
Close to a Beautiful Point,
Pacing Patience up the Wall...
Keep Calm,
Read Your Psalms
And Quran...
Kiss him gently ,
He's fashioned from water and mud,
But acts like Steel,
But he's molten butter under the
Right Touch of
Love...

99 ATTRIBUTES

* Why You ?*

She said, why you doing this to me, why you stretching me thin, why you playing your violin with the strings of my heart, now my hips are full of your Song...

Why you call my name, why we think the same , why you take the blame , when I'm as guilty as you, and if these sticks and stones don't break your bones, I'm sure my heart will do, I'm so weak for you, you think you're Strong....

Why you bring me here, why you lock me up, why you till my soil and plant your seeds, why you water me softly and flood my heart, why you acting shy when you're so boldly taking charge, why you blow me kisses and take my Breath...

Why you write those poems, why you sweeten your words, why you open my sky and swing my bird , why you pulling back so I can chase you down, why this cat and mouse when I purr for you, why you standing here when you said you Left ...

99 ATTRIBUTES

Why you just won't leave, why you pull me back , why you want this pain, why you acting sprung but I feel the sprain, why you speak of love when you hurt like this , why the truth or dare when you know the risk, why you tempt me so, why you lick those
Lips ...

Why you want me now, why you touching deep, why you lift my dress with the slightest smile, why you spill my knees, why you swim in me, why you drown me out when you don't even speak, why you whisper words I can't repeat, and why you won't answer...
So I Asked Her,
Why we meet in Dreams
and Fields of
Green...

99 ATTRIBUTES

* Where Truth Lies *

One of my Truths told a Lie...
And When I find Her,
I'll make Her Confess in a Heartbreak
Full of
Why...
I know how Guilty this Looks,
But if She would just clear my Name,
I Swear I would take the Blame...
Let's just say it was Abel who Murdered
Cain,
Now that Switches up the whole
Game,
The Silence of The Lamb and The Screams
of the
Vegetables ,
She fell into my Crockpot Poetry to Sweeten
the
Taste,
But I added so
much Baby Fat to it,
it'll widen your waist and gain your
Weight
And Robust Hips
Look even better with
Her
Face,
One of my Lies found The
Truth ,

99 ATTRIBUTES

As innocent as She looks,
She's as
Guilty
as
You...

99 ATTRIBUTES

* Somali Butterfly *

I Crushed a Sweet Little Somali Butterfly
Acting Cute and Playing Pretty
She was born in the Garden but
Raised in the
City,
She got Rug Burns from Prayers
And Shea Butter Conversations to
Smooth over the Harsh Reality of
A Beautiful Lie with the Sky Blue Ugly
Truth ....
Oh Really???
She's so Picky, after Tupac Died, She
stopped listening to Biggie,
I don't know how she remembers that
Because she was so Itty Bitty,
Just around the size of a Penny,
But She was that Loyal that her
Devotion was never
Iffy,
She had her Contradictions like Lipstick and
Eye Shadow as if She really needed that,
She was Yellow Black with Blue Bone
Roots, Yemen Branches and a Lap fit for
Persian
Kitties,

99 ATTRIBUTES

Kissy Kissy, I Feel like The Arabian Prince
singing Darling Little Prissy, I must be
Dreaming, I mean what was I Thinking,
Crushing a Somali Butterfly
Like things wouldn't get
Sticky...

99 ATTRIBUTES

* More Than Valentines *

You can't squeeze my Love into a Day, write it on a card or bundle it inside 12 roses, can't box my love like chocolate, nor table it as a dinner for two in a crowded restaurant, no pocket book romance, a penny for your thoughts and a dollar for your Heart...
My Love is Timeless, reaching into cosmic eons, bending space and time, digging worm holes into the fabric of atoms punching black holes to inhale universal love and breathe life out of the other side, Love is the Endless Start...

My Love is a wordless poem, traveling where words don't exist into voiceless expressions that screams through soundless echoes heard through a touch that ripples through the honey ponds of the Soul, dripping off the tongue with sweetness soaking in Her
Ears...
My Love is a Flower garden cultivated in the soil of kisses rooted core deep into the hot springs of Earth body, mountain highs and valley lows, river flows and ocean depths , emotional rip tides, drowning in mud pies to seed sunflowers that pull the sky closer than

99 ATTRIBUTES

Near...

My Love is Chocolate spill and finger licks under twilight cinnamon skies you can taste it in the air like a gulp of midnight milky-way, water-falling off your chin into a whirlpool of coco skin, I'm your Chocolate kind , making a mess between your lips and fingers til I melt puddles in your Thighs...
My Love is a balcony Dinner for Two, overlooking the black sand of beachfront love waves crashing into our toes like spilling wine from our hearts over sauteed plated kisses with dessert pie in your eyes, I can't help but spoon feed this love on the yumminess that hungers for a priceless Love that spends every dime of my Time...
Because our everyday Love, is more than Valentines...

99 ATTRIBUTES

* One of These Days *

One of these days like Now, I'm going to
kiss you where it counts,
Where wounded Women are medicated on
Poetry,
my words may sting a little, and these lips
will make you say Ouch...

Don't let my Shea Butter Smooth fool you,
I'm as Rugged as any Carpet laid over this
Hard Wood Floor in hopes that you will
roast your toes in the Passions of my
FirePlace ,
Between your chin and collarbone I want to
kiss your neck like a Violin symphony
having an epiphany with a hickie that
monkey bit my own Lips, tongue brushing a
Blush upon your Face...

Lets meet between your eyelashes on the
cliffs of your wetlands , if your tears are
Oceans, so then your Eyes must be Pearls,
The windows to your Soul, Behold the
Treasure that can't be
Stole...

In the Mist of Still Water Ponds you Rest
Easy in Gardens busy with Life and Beauty,
Perfumed Butterflies , Two Sliccs of Moon
and Green leaf Sun Tea , just to wash down

99 ATTRIBUTES

your Smile so I can stomach your Happiness
and Belch my Own...

One of these days like Now, I'm going to
kiss you where it counts ...
Right there Smack in the Middle of your
Smile...

99 ATTRIBUTES

* Moroccan Mint Tea *

She dressed in Seven Layers of Heaven
And Sun Spun Silk,
As Modest as the Moon dressed in
Mink Marbled Midnight with her Smile
Dipped in Milk,
Her Prayers were written on her hands
in Henna and Perfumed with her
Breath,
She Spoke of Belief and Beauty and Dates
for Breakfast but couldn't answer how many
Kisses She had
Left,
If I could just steal her Breath, I would never
Return her Lips, like a sip of Moroccan Mint
Tea over the Balcony of her
Eyelashes,
She was Bashful enough to let me Dream
In Saltless Oceans in the middle of The
Sahara Desert diving into Wet Sand,
Tickling her with my
Splashing...

99 ATTRIBUTES

* Every Tomorrow *

Every Tomorrow I kiss your lips from inside your mouth,
So you can taste our future every time you swallow,
I want to plant seeds in your belly til they bloom in your womb as chocolate morsels delightful
Every Tomorrow,

Let's take a trip to the Moon with fishing poles and catch starfish, and throw them into the night sky to glitter the dark with illuminating love clusters ,
Every Tomorrow,

I want to Borrow more future, with more laughs and less Sorrow,
Every Tomorrow,

I count my blessings by the hairs on your head, and with so many hair styles I may be awhile, you giggle, " you silly"..and I still made you smile :-)
Every Tomorrow,..

it's been my pleasure to measure your soul Blush against the canvas of the universe ,
In this cosmic dance, I want to Father your time, if you will Mother my Earth,

99 ATTRIBUTES

Every Tomorrow,

I'm kicking away yesterday, Loving you
Fresh and Anew ,
Powder blue skies dripping honey ripe sun
onto your tongue and I can taste you too,..
Every Tomorrow,

I want to ask you out on a first date with a
lump in my throat and sweat in my palms
and more determined than ever to have you
as my Every Tomorrow...

99 ATTRIBUTES

* Veiled Moon *

From behind the Veil of Virgin
Guilt and Voluptuous
Eyes,
As Vulnerable as a Vanity Vase
Decorated on Both
Sides,
Silk Soul Dressed in Egyptian Cotton Cool,
Venus Rule under Pregnant Moon and
Crystal
Lagoons,
Gentle Storms rolling in rivers of Onyx
Swirl,
Runaway Girl Trapped inside of a Woman,
backing into the
World,
With a Womb full of Future raging in
Gardens watered in
Tears,
Spring Bruises and Crushed Lilies into the
Capital City of Asmara where the Four
Winds meet to Breeze Secrets through your
Ears,
I've Never Seen Beauty so Tender with
Ancient Rhythms around and about your
Hips,
Speaking of you,
I was saving this for a
Kiss...

99 ATTRIBUTES

* Tempted Poetry *

Don't Tempt me with Poetry,
I'm nowhere as Strong as these
Words,
I don't win these Fights,
If you pen me Down, I'll never Write my way out of
This,
I will be ridiculed for all my Misspelled
Truths,
My Grammatical errors are so glaring ,
It's like I ain't caring ,
Weather you see me rain over my own
Parade ....
She may leave me Blank like my
Last
Page
And ask me to write things
I could never
Say...
I'm telling you...
Don't Tempt me with this
Poetry...
I'll reWrite your
Story...
And Start You
Where
I

99 ATTRIBUTES

End...
So where should we
Begin...?

99 ATTRIBUTES

{ Throwback Thursday }

* The Old Woman Said # 13 *

The Old Woman said,
Love is forever, Kisses are for Life and Heartbreak is a Season,
She said the Pretty in Young Women is a fleeting thing,
Why not find her Beauty which no face is capable of holding and latch on to that,
She said the Beautiful things are such, that one must become it to enjoy it,
And don't touch a Woman where it hurts , being that she is a Butterfly with a Scorpions tail , and Her Poison will make you forget her Sweets...

The Old Woman said, you Men haven't amounted to half of my Father, and yet my Fathers dreams haven't reached half of the things you've Seen,
So why not Measure yourselves with greater strength and resolve , and be more than the Past,..only look back to Smile, but Keep Forward, because God Bless The Child that Grows in The Now,
Sure we used to swim in the Nile,
built Pyramids and Discovered Ourselves, But that was our Times,
You are Responsible for your Times,

99 ATTRIBUTES

Don't fall off the Clock,
Cherish your Days, Minutes and Second
Hand Tics... Or just go Stand in the Sun and
watch your Shadow count for you...

The Old Woman said be gentle with your
Children, they tear so easy , keep'um in a
safe place and guard them with Love, so that
when you become their Child, they'll guard
you with the same
Love...

The Old Woman said Love is forever, Kisses
are for Life and Heartbreak is for a Season...
So ain't no sense in y'all crying like its the
End...

99 ATTRIBUTES

Wanna Fall in Love?

I heard you wanna fall in Love, well let me give you that extra push and pull the roses from under your feet tipping over cream-soda waterfalls I don't mean to burst your bubbles and fish your water for troubles but this here Love ain't for the delicate of heart because dreams are sugarcoated nightmares, you wake this monster and you better be prepared to defend this sandcastle against a tsunami wave, because a heartless swim will drown you in one
Gulp...

Every rose has its thorn and paper hearts are torn trying to piece this poem back together keeping my hands bloody with ink so I'm'a warn you with the trumpets of chapped lips and lip busting kisses, cows tripping over moons and spilling milk over cries, fellas there's a jealous girl in town , a new edition to this condition, fresh as a mint with pretty brown eyes, thinking she ready to jump into the heart of the matter and splatter this love against the walls of her soul, this is still truth or dare, it'll run you across The State-Line to Elope ....

99 ATTRIBUTES

It'll break every bone in your tongue and
make your knees come splashing down,.
have you walking on clouds and snacking on
stars, drinking sun like ice tea on a hot
winter night under a potbelly moon that eats
through the night sharing her last with dawn
who offers you the best piece of day... And if
you listen close you will hear the cries of
broken hearted lovers with deep moaning
and wailing and it behooves you to
remember every smile is the half sister of a
cry, same Momma different daddies so you
can imagine how they get along,.. This here
is for the Strong because it will make you
crawl on the belly of tears swearing never to
love again.. You wanna fall in this..
I suggest you stand in This
and fight with your last breath because it
going to take that before your collapse and
perhaps you may find a heart to rescue you
from all the foolishness you
Spoke...

99 ATTRIBUTES

* Our Old Ways *

We don't kiss like we use to,
What happened to those lips that use to burn down our tongues and leave our mouths
Smoking,
We don't touch like we use to,
What happened to those hands, Feely, Frisky and Fondling , a Tender Touch to Torch our bodies and leave us quivering like blanket beach cuddles with our toes in the
Ocean....
We don't talk like we use to,
What happened to those Consenting Conversations Caressing our Conscious Confirmations, Concerns and Comforts , I Can't Call it , but Damn, it's like we don't got anything to say or afraid to say what's really under the
Silence,
We don't laugh like we use to,
What happened to those Goofy, Stop I'm'a Pee on myself,
So Silly and Cracking Up til our Sides Hurt, like we can't Front, this ain't so Funny anymore like Miss Celie's Smile, ducking and
Hiding...
We don't look at each other like we use to,
What happened to those, Sultry, Seductive Stares, Stuck on Stupid and Lost in LaLa

99 ATTRIBUTES

Land, Scared to Blink and Miss a Moment, can't take our eyes away, they just wanna play in each others Soul, but now things just don't Look the
Same,
We don't love like we use to,
What happened to those Feelings of Passion, Dashing through the Corridors of Ecliptic Twirling and Wobbling Whoas !!!! So Dizzy and Doused in upside down Happiness, can't catch our Breath like I could just Die Right Now, Feels like Flowers Growing in my Smile, and You So Damn Sexy, like a Silky Moon slipping in and out of the Clouds, Porch Light Kisses,
I'm Missing those Nights in these Lonely Days, I Long for Our Old
Ways...

99 ATTRIBUTES

* Lip Balm-Bay *

It's never been easy on my lips,
I've tasted salted kisses with a dash of lemon,
A stinging touch will tuck a bottom lip,
Chapped blood suck,
Screaming Ouch and Fukc!!!
With Cuts that'll debone a Kiss, like a deflated Pout,
She didn't have to take it out on my Mouth like that,
These were made for Sugar Smacks,
Kiss me and I'll Kiss you back,
But don't act like Lipstick and stand between us,
Because I'll Smear that into Runoff , and make you Come Off like Pillow Talk and replenish you like
Lipgloss,
I'm Lip Balm-Bay,
They call me
Big Lip Truth,
If you only knew what these Two have been Through,
You would Lick'um too,
They've been,
Bit, Busted, Blamed, Bronzed, Blessed and Brought to the
Brothel to Bargain with prostitutes with Pussy on my

99 ATTRIBUTES

Breath, and I didn't Break a Smile because I
was tired of Being Broke,
So they took me to the Bahamas and
Baptized me on Black Sand Beaches,
I ain't Bashful no more,
I got Blueberries and Buckwheat,
Budging out like Buddhas Big Belly,
I kiss like an Ole' Country Boy Bumpkin,
Making you go Bubblegum
Bonkers,
But at the end of the Day when I collect it
all and Pray,
These lips are Bowed with
Bismillah....

99 ATTRIBUTES

* Goodbye Hello *

We've said goodbye so many times that now it's become hello, how are you, how have you been, think we ought to try this again?....
We can't be that foolish , we've read this love story again and again , from beginning to end, ain't no happily ever afters, hop scotching   hand in hand into the blood orange sunset of our passion promises ,
Crashing into broken Hearts, a wasted love, spent too soon, Doomed from the concept of a Dream time interrupted by wake up alarms,
But we press snooze , and let our hearts drift on the soul waters of our cosmic cruise into the boundless limitations of our imagination ,
Blissfully absent from reality, this insanity and emotional madness , trying to correct the butterfly effect , I can't protect you from me, if I'm
Imprisoned in you , I'm in the belly of the beautiful, tortured by what could've been and terrorized by love songs, and we thought we had it all , if so we lost it all, while still grasping at the clouds of our Dream Love hopelessly perplex as to what to do next, too many goodbyes becomes hellos , so we gotta let go, turn our backs and don't look back,

99 ATTRIBUTES

lest we become pillars of salt that has lost it's flavor,, no hugs, no tender kisses, no dancing eyes, no call me laters, this is our farewell love... Goodbye Hello...

Bleeding Heart

I'm into her, and she meant to do that,
peeling back the scab on my heart....
OUCH!!!!... Damn you Woman!!!
And Her Apology was,
You had that
Coming.....
Gotta Love it,
The way she spun it,
Like turning tables and having breakfast for
dinner,
I wasn't able to pull back, so I pull her into
all
My
Loving...
Kissing Cousins and Punching Nephews, I'm
just so Happy to be in Love, I'm giving
Charlie Horses and Monkey Bites
...
She like, Stop Shabazz,
You Play
Too
Much...
Naw... You had that Coming,
Tugging on my Heart,
I should rip your Thighs apart, Curl your
Toes until your Hip Bones explode and Bust
your
Water
Balloon...

99 ATTRIBUTES

BOOM!!!
Yeah I'm'a do it just like That,.. She said careful now,
Don't throw out your back....
Shit I'm'a throw my back out, my phone out and my mind out,... Just to be
Stupid with it....
She giggled and said, you a Fool for that, And I'm
Fool enough to burn your toes on the Sun, while Pushing you Happy over the stars on a Swinging
Moon...
Yeah I meant to do that...
Thanks for picking my
Bleeding
Heart...
You can Wet your
Kisses in it
Now...

99 ATTRIBUTES

* Back Turning on Love *

You think you can turn your back on my heart,.. I'll burn your memory down at every turn, play me for a violin and I'll turn the music up so
loud...

I'll drown out everything you've ever said, I'll rip your pictures in my mind and shred every thought of you, Oh you thought my love was just pregnant moons, giggling butterflies and over the rainbow splashing smiles, don't let the ladybugs on my shoulders fool you, because those mean bitches think I'm too soft in love anyhow,...

And they're just waiting for me to turn them into fire breathing dragons to burn these sand castles to the ground so they can resurrect the Phoenix in me and bury the falcon in an unmarked grave, I'll wipe these kisses with shit paper and flush them out of my soul and make doves cry rivers under the heart hanging gallows of a love once Cherished....

You think you can turn your back on my heart,...I'll tear every feather out of your back til you bleed like the passion of Christ

99 ATTRIBUTES

and I won't forgive this sin if it cost me heaven,
hell has no fury like that of a Poet who has had his heart slammed in the sliding doors of love, and I gave you the keys to these locks and broke you out of your chains , I'm the BraveHeart of these Love Legions on the frontline taking arrows in the heart for you, and you betray me like lipstick Judas, your beautifully flawed self has broke mirrors and now you can't hide in these reflections I see inside your nakedness , if this was just pussy, pleasure and pain,
I would've packed my bags for the last flirt who told me my sky was under her skirt, but this was deeper than touch and feel, this was no hands no lips, just pure soul bliss and now I gotta watch you walk out on what our hearts said would never
Perish...

* Again *

I wanna try you all over again ,
this time I wanna butter you on both sides ,
Slap you on your cinnamon buns and make
your sugar go
Ouch!!!
Its like a Beautiful morning going rough on
the Stars,
You can't hold your glitter together,
Here let me glue you to this Kiss..
Now doesn't that
Feel a whole lot
Better...
I'm sure we can frolic in the faith and in the
fever of that fact,
That I just don't know how to act around
you,
I start kicking mountains over and ripping
the sky apart, throwing a tantrum just to
whisper something
Like...
Can
We
Do
That
Again...

99 ATTRIBUTES

* Breakup Poem *

I broke up with a Poem,
She had her reasons for leaving too,
Said I was too possessive and jealous,
She couldn't hang out with her Pens without me thinking they were up to something written and forbidden ,
I mean She maintained her periods ,
But there were so many question marks,
Adjectives and Run-on Sentences,
And the Ambiguity of words she couldn't explain ,
Left us with a half written page...
We had all the ink in the world and Canons of Closet Drama with Connotations of meaning more than we ever said,...
She said I was the Most Beautiful Poet she ever read,
So right in the Heart
yet so
wrong in the Head,
We could've been such a Lovely Couplet,
but she was so wrong for the Stage and so write in the Bed,
And there she goes with her attitude,
"You don't own the Copyrights to me!!!"...
"I can say whatever I want, dress however I like , be a freak with the spoken word poets

99 ATTRIBUTES

and masturbate in front of an audience with the mic"....
Talkin like that, We don't got nothing else to write about,
We can crumble these paper hearts and end this ink where Love Notes can't get a word in...
She'll never feel My
Pen again,
Cold part about it , her words were paper thin ,
So this is my apologia
To
a
Poem
I
Had
to
End...

99 ATTRIBUTES

* The Old Woman Said # 1 *

The Old Woman said,
Keep your Friends close, your Enemies closer and your Woman closest ,...
because She's the hostess of my Soul, with invitations and hospitality of Beauty and Southern Charm like a boatload of Children, Good Cooking and Porch Swing Conversations through silent nights that the crickets interrupt , these moonlit moments mean the most when we soak into each others eyes, and spill out of our thighs ,..
We hold hands but touch with our Hearts, drown our toes in the pond after summer breeze walks through the park under butterfly shade and sometimes we swim through the sky just to get our moonlight tans on the beaches of the Sun, and we swear by these Kisses, that it's something deeper than sprung,.. It's Sprang, inside flower gardens where
the Lovebirds Sang, splashing in Happiness like April Rain under pregnant clouds and rainbow Pains,
We keep birthing Smiles, like the New Born Kisses of a Honey Child,..
Never mind me, I'm just up to my eyelashes in Emotions, floating on the Wisdom of the

99 ATTRIBUTES

Old Woman   who said, Keep your Friends
close , your Enemies closer and your
Woman
Closest...

99 ATTRIBUTES

* Sad Sillies *

Cosmopolitan Woman,
Walking Across Ancient Ruins,
Slumped Cities
and
Crocheted Cultures,
Stepping over Drunken Soldiers,
Summers are Colder,
and
Children are Older,
Her Lips are Sober,
Can't Drink Whine at a Time like This,
Men take advantage of a Kiss and end up
with their mouths under Unforgiving
Hips,
Roses are Red and Violence is
Blue,
The Abuse of Women start with a Kick in
the
Womb,
And a Knife in the Heart,
A Walk in The Park,
A Song in the Dark
And a Good Woman with
a Scarf,
Could Never get
Use to These
Loose Cities,

99 ATTRIBUTES

She was Wrapped too Tight,
Traded the Moon for
City Lights,
and Sad Sillies...

99 ATTRIBUTES

* Careful Love *

She ain't so different than me,
We look kinda cute together,
We laugh at the same sillies,
And Really enjoy romantic comedies ,
This is probably the Craziest thing we've ever done,
We unplugged The Sun, and dipped the Moon in Chocolate, got riddled with Shooting Stars and said this is a Good Night to Die for Love,
And Shot each other in the Heart...
Like Oh My...
I didn't know it would be
So painful...
Here... Let me Kiss That....
Shit who would've thought Love could Hurt...
I ain't so different than her...
I'm just more tender
Now...

99 ATTRIBUTES

* Calling You *

Pretty Things don't always come in Blue,
Sometimes they come in
You,
With a Twist of Raspberry
Soul
Under Apple Green Skin with
Flakes of
Gold,
Air Spun Sillies, with Smiles Poppin'
Wheelies,
I'm like Really, I left my Fingerprints in you,
You can't tell me you don't
Feel Me,
I'm so Touchy, TAG...
You're It,
Chase that Thought into the Corners of your
Mind and don't worry about making
Sense,
Let's just make it Fit, like Slim Chances and
High School Dances,
I waited all night for the Last Slow Jam,..So
don't leave me
Standing,
I'm better at Falling, I ain't Walking or
Crawling,
I'm just Chocolate Puddle,
So go Ahead and Answer,
That's Me
Calling...

99 ATTRIBUTES

* Ruin a Rose *

This is no way to Ruin a Rose,
and Roll over Rain
Rattle a Rottweiler
and Lose Reason to
Rage,
We got No Room to Run
Like a Cat Surrounded by
Ratchet Hood Rats Pulling
Rank Drinking on Captain Morgan's
Rum,
Sh!t just got Real Stank,
It's Getting Late, Why You Gotta be Here
After Floetry Broke Up, and My Poetry
Spoke Up,
I don't got any Heart Left to
Break,
Your Guess is as Good as
Mine, Your Breath was just as
Morning as Mine, Your Love was just as
Damaged as Mine,
Being that you were all about Yours,
I had to look after
Mine,
Now Baby Hold On,
This is No Way to Ruin a Rose
and Roll over Rain,
Put the Water Gun Down
Who can survive bullets of

99 ATTRIBUTES

Tears, Point it my way,
I deserve
The
Pain...

99 ATTRIBUTES

* Living Poetry *

I come from where the Sun rain smiles on my tears, where the Women dance in the brightest colors polishing rainbows between their hips and Children's laughter tickles the ocean deep skies an honest Blue...

We build houses with no doors because our freedom doesn't cage, we bathe in butterflies and eat kisses for breakfast with flower filled bellies, we burp jasmine giggles and drink morning
Dew...

We make love between half eaten moons and pregnant mountains , Women birth stars and Men build heavens to support them while Music plays us to the tunes of
Life...

We don't have a thing to say because we keep doing what we are.. The Children of The Sun flower the world in Love and when we do speak...it's Poetry... We're too busy living to
Write...

* Tears of a Ladybug *

When sweet turns sour on lemon puckered lips and sea salt kisses and it hurts enough to squeeze a tear from a ladybug remember the lovers quarrel and the silence that fell over the unspoken screams that shattered whine glasses like heartbreak opera , but all She remembers is his laughter and butter melting
Smile...

99 ATTRIBUTES

* More Than Friends *

Wasn't we suppose to be friends , platonic, no lip line crossing, like we can talk about anything,
I treat you like a God-Sister with a Helluva Krush, trying not to touch or wake up my Dream,
We do this feather weight flirting, sure to arch eyebrows, and you like,..Girl, That's Shabazz, he like my Brother,
We stuck between what if and preserving our friendship, under a night filled sky of shooting atlantic starrs, like secret lovers,
Talking about you wish you could find a man like me, and I need a Woman like you, but I hide that under my Breath,
With a stick of juicy fruit that I broke in half to share with you, chewing on this feeling I'm trying to Confess,
I release these nerves in laughter and wishing I didn't have to hear about the guys that like you, but I play it off with, He Ain't your Type ,
You call me a Charmer, a Conscious Ladies Man is just asking for trouble and what a Brother like you need is a Good Wife,

99 ATTRIBUTES

I thought you would never ask, :-) .... Oh, but it's me who should be purposing with a heart full of roses, throwing my caution to the
Wind,
So when we gonna stop playing and start saying.., We wanna be More Than Friends...

99 ATTRIBUTES

* The Endless Poem *

I want to Start a Poem that Ends with You,
Drown you in my Ink like Ocean Blues,
Blur you between these Lines and let You Soak on Through,
Ring out this Paper, Like Look what you Made Me Do,
It's like Words for Chocolate, So let your Sweet Tooth Chew,
Paper Spitballs of Peppermint, I'm Sweet and Nasty Too,
Like Black Ink Kisses, I gotta Write To You,
Secrets of A Love Note Diary for Open Mic Confessions who could hide this Truth,
In a Room full of Pens and Paper, They Like,
Girl He Must Be Talking to You,
You're Kinda Shy, but you know I couldn't End this Poem without it Starting over With You....

99 ATTRIBUTES

* I'll Be In Touch *

Why are all the Good Women married or taken just like you,
Runaway bride meet me on the other side of your vows, where I say , I Do...

In the fantasies of my heart , I imagine dancing with you in our home on hard wood floors after wining in the dining room just across the starlit patio, happy giggling feet as lovers twirl... You should've been my girl...

I should've meet you at the Farmers market, watching you taste the local strawberries In your sun dress,... I confess, I wanted to meet all that yumminess on your lips, and pick you ripe and fresh,
I'll Introduce myself as goose bumps running up your neck with a sweet whisper at the drip of your earlobe , Oh how I want to taste you just like that strawberry, gently bite down into your sweetness ,
Imagine us meeting this way with the summer breeze playing in your dress as we share plums and peaches ,
Can we share a conversation on a moonlit beach, as we braid our fingers together while aiming at shooting stars and journey the

99 ATTRIBUTES

expanse of our dreams on the back of comets...

Distant Lover,
I should've been your Lover, I should've shouldered your tears and tickled you silly under the covers,
Foreplay til four in the morning, making love on the thread of dawn to brighten the sun as it rushes it's nosy self over the mountains and into our window, making sweat beads of glitter as I deliver you into the euphoric ecstasy exclusively erotic indulgment of you and I...

If you don't mind, I gotta say what's on my mind,.. I know I'm running too late and out of time as you have already arrived as someone else's valentine,
But if you were mine and not his, it would be him saying these things and it would be me blackening his eye...

So maybe next life time on the other side of our hearts rainbow, you'll find me in your childhood, teasing you , pulling on your braids as proof evident of my crush, I'll be hiding just beneath your blush coming of age with your touch,... And if I can say this much,
I'll Be In Touch...

99 ATTRIBUTES

* Love Reloaded *

Remember me, the one who fell out of the tree of life just to land on the pillows of your kisses,
How have you been?, you look good, like home cooked comfort food, and I wanna help you wash those dishes ,
Share a dream with you over candle lit soul conversations on the balcony of a lovers promise,
As I serenade you under our first blue moon, as the orange sky waves goodbye like the farewell of a comet,
Can we braid our fingers til we can't pull apart , blow butterflies out of our bellies and illuminate the dark,
Under the skylight of your love I found everything I was searching for,
Through birth and re-birth , I have traveled in worm holes just because I dig you to your Earth core,
I wanna listen to those   hummingbirds recite you poetry til your ears honey drip,
And splash all over your last tear with a sweeter smile dancing on your lips,
I am falling while standing next to you deeper into your hearts embrace,
You write love letters on your face as I read your smile and listen to your eyes and the Beautiful things they say,

99 ATTRIBUTES

Like... kiss me, hold me, love me, show me,... Hear me, Know me, and I've done exactly like you told me,
With bunches of kisses, and soul licking, making out in the back seats of our hearts , Parked on the cliffs of our souls in the chocolate taste of our dark,
Can I pull the moon out of your smile so I can watch the shadows dance the lovers ensemble across your body's naked soul as I kiss the curves of your hips,.. With these lips I hold,
You with my last breath, you're my last dance of the night , hold on extra tight , bite if you have to,
as I krush groove your hips, you melt just as I grab you, splashing all over me in a milky way,
Come closer still and fall into my chest, climb up my arms, whisper in my ear and dive into my heart in a silky way,
Do you feel that ? goosebumps tickle up your back, nibble on your ears, and lick around your neck with crawling kisses on the wet, Do you feel that?
Embrace me in the cool of the garden as we squeeze tasty sun drops between our tongues , you taste like home..
We all alone in a crowded room, let's set this fire with a kiss in the cool....

99 ATTRIBUTES

We're everywhere we need to be, standing here in the middle of the sweet,
It's everything to you and me,
I'm back in Love, you're back with me,
I'm flying high like moonrise summer nights,
Til they stand us on a cake and announce us husband and wife...
This is our Love Reloaded ...

99 ATTRIBUTES

* Cool with Me *

We're not like we use to be,
Maybe you just got use to me,
Maybe it's the Routine, and The
Same Ole' Usually,
We do Less Touching and More
Silence, Maybe you're just Finding
Yourself and
Losing Me,
I got enough Clues to see,
So don't try to get Cute with me,
This is the Part Where you get to
Do to me,
Everything you said He did to you,
So finally you get to
Ruin me,
So When She finds me like who would
Throwaway such a Good Man,
That goes Perfect with her New
Shoes,
She like Girl I ain't No Fool,
Maybe He didn't fit your Look,
But He goes
Cool with Me...

99 ATTRIBUTES

* Music to your Thighs *

It's such a thelonious symphony between you and I,
Composed under hip bone rhythms and kisses that trumpet melodies of lovers duets and sexy ensembles as my fingers play piano on your collarbones to your soprano moans over a septet of jazz riffs and Coltrane thigh
quivers,
Stolen moments between the broken time of drum beats that the heart can't help but to waltz to, and I've been easy on your double time feel, eight to the bar, give me another inch and I'll take a Miles Davis up your scales and have you screaming blue notes that'll shatter a wine bottle after we sip and slip out of these clothes,
I'm'a make you spill it from your toes, under my cool we can make the moon drool us a pool of honey-nut passion ballads to soak this wetness in and ring your belly out into an interlude of soul claps and finger snaps between your knees you hold my long trombone with saxophone strokes and you can whistle your clarinet til you curl your lips, because you've been music to my soul with every scent trapped inside this Kiss...Now play that song between your Thighs...

* Butter Bones *

How many Love Songs must we dance to
before the
Ensemble
Begins ....
Before the Butter melts over Buttermilk and
Butter Bones, and you Butter Be ready to
slide outta
your
Skin....

You're Plush Pretty on the Beautiful Side of
Things, don't wanna hurt your Smile, but let
me wipe that lipstick off with a
Kiss....
Did you taste that,
like pearls popping in your mouth and silver
licks of Moon...Yummy isn't it...Catch a
Butterfly with your Eyelashes and hold me
in a
Glimpse....

Hold still ... Don't blink...
Now open your mouth...Sink...
Let's wet this drink and drown upside down
in the deep end of the
Sky....
I wanna cover you,
Smuggle you...
And run off to the edge of the

99 ATTRIBUTES

World ...
Ready, Set, Go... Let's leap over the Sun and Roast these toes in Cosmic Cuddles, Draped in Dark Matter like Murky Jazz Enclaves Let's keep Grooving til we pull down our Thighs...

99 ATTRIBUTES

* Ain't Never Lied *

Ain't no Woman ever lied on me,
So believe everything she says,
Like he ain't Right in the Head, and He can't go wrong in the
Bed,
He eat his burgers without Bread and his Closest friends
Are
Dead,
He so hard on Women with all that he Understands,
So Possessive and Controlling, he just so Afraid she didn't mean all that she
Said,
He's all Heart and Soul, Poems and Pencil Lead,
Drawing his life in the sand,
Trying to wash away his pain in Ocean Storms of Emotions But that's what gives him his
Edge,
He got his Fathers Charm and His Momma's Caution and Lost Touch with his Best Friend
Fred,
He like Beautiful Women with an Ugly Past and he only eats as much Pussy as you give
Head,
So Afraid of being cheated for playing Fair,

99 ATTRIBUTES

He like his Woman with Natural Hair, Nappy,
Wavy, Curly,
Short or Long, he really don't care,
He's more concerned with what's in your
Head,
What you Think,
And
The Last Book you Read...
Afros , Braids and Swinging Dreads,
He like his Women,
Black, Brown, Yellow and Red,
He talks to himself while pacing in circles,
We call him
Rain
Man,
He's the inbred of Heartbreak and Catch me
if you
Can,
He fled the scene of the Rhyme,
And told his Truth as
Poetry
Instead ,
Like I said,... Ain't no Woman ever lied on
me,
But they'll take the 5th to protect me,
He's just Crazy For Love,
And He Don't take his
Meds...

* Kisses Do Lie *

She looked Him in the eye and wrapped a smile over Her lie, didn't even ruffle an eyelash, how beautifully did She get ugly, like menstrual blood on a wedding dress or a kiss that sends a Prophet to his
Death...

He dug love from under His finger nails with His hands in Her soil He thought He could plant gardens, but sucking green thumbs doesn't make everything rosy like the morning scent of a petals
Breath...

The morning sickness of a pregnant Heart can miscarriage a stillborn Love and He didn't believe in abortions , so they would just have to grow up fast and bury the past under the moons quarter
Crest...

Kisses Do Lie and that's just the Truth of it so lipstick that across your smooches ,
She stained His collar
and
Bow-tied Her Love around His neck but He still held Her by the stomach under Her
Dress...

~ So Touchy ~

She had a Troubled Love and Her
Smile had a rough Upbringing,
Her Father wasn't Faithful and Her
Momma was Faithless, She didn't Trust
Words for being
Pretty Ugly,
But there was always Make Up and
Forgiveness at the end of every Friday
And at the Start of every Heartbreak,
there's always the Promise
of I'm not like the
Others, as Picky as Any Choosy Lover,
You can even ruin Sugar with Too
Much
Honey,
She let Her Tears Down Easy and didn't
Demand too much of her Heart, It wouldn't
survive another Kiss, So she swore Never to
Betray her own Lips,
She felt Sorry for her Soul,
Which appealed through her Eyes,
If you could just
Touch Me...

* NASTY WRITE *

She said Write me a Nasty Poem,
With your Nasty Pen,
I got some Nasty Paper
Wanna hear my Nasty Sins,
So then Write me
a Nasty Note,
Talk Nasty and Take it out on my Nasty
Throat,
We just some Nasty Folks
Reading between the lines of What Nasty
Wrote,
She said, You So Nasty Boo,
You got a Nasty Cool,
I'll be your Nasty Fool,
Because you're just as
Nasty Too,
Come Spend a Nasty Night
I'll be your Nasty Wife,
She said, You know I Keep it Nasty Tight,
I Said... You know You're
Nasty Write?...

* Perfect High *

She was a Dope Poem,
Strung Out in The Back
Alleys of Paper
Dolls,
She was Hooked on the Ink and got Pimp'd
by the Pen,
Stuck on that Boy, pent down by her Panties
and
Bras...

Gin and Junkie Juice,
Jezebel's Juggernaut,
She's Been Jammin'
that Jelly in her
Jugular since a
Juvenile,
She ain't Dead, She's just Dope, Like
WHOA,
She even Mixes Ink with
her Coke, On Some Realest Sh!t I Ever
Wrote,
She got a Break in her Soul and a Crack in
her
Smile...

Heartbreak Poems,
take it to the edge of the
Paper, Jumping off into the
Fire for an Ether Burn on a Soiled Mattress,

99 ATTRIBUTES

Overdose Dreaming of
White Paper and
Blue Lines,
She had a Jones for
Poets,
So Who was I to Question her
Life,
While selling her my Writes
for the
Prefect
High...

* Hookah Kisses *

She packed her Hookah with BubbleGum,
And Blew Soul Bubbles with
AirPocket Kisses,
Hoping I can Pop One and Fall Apart in the
Smoke,
While Swinging in her Clouds of
Now,
I got a Mouthful of
Poetry,
Praying I don't
Choke...
I broke my Paper and Crumbled my
Pen...
I can't say none of what I
Wrote...
I'm soaking in the Night Breeze
Between Her
Lips
And
Hookah
Smoke ...

99 ATTRIBUTES

~ Falcon Fly ~

I don't just want to cross your Mind, I
want to sit with you at the rivers of your
thoughts with our feet soaking in the Sky
and
Laughter jumping on our Thighs,
A Belly Full Butterflies
And Apples for Eyes
I want to Rollover Time
And Squeeze Forever out of
The Other Side,
Loop our Lips like Happy
Hour with a Slice of
Lime,
We ain't just Drunk in Love, when you're
As Junkie as us, you'll find yourself
Snorting Poetic
Lines,
I Swear I ain't never been
This High,
Got you Looking
Where The
Falcon
Fly...

99 ATTRIBUTES

* Was it the Part ? *

Which part of I LOVE YOU, didn't you understand...
Was it the part when I kissed you and took a can opener to my heart so I could open up and bleed emotions for you...

Was it the part when I slammed my finger in the door for a wedding ring and the throbbing pain of sensitivity to the things that hurt but that I found worth it for you...

Was it the part when I made your children mine, shared the stressing and blessings of growing pain with moments of bone stretching ouch, he ain't your daddy but he damn sure is your father, just look at how he do for them and you...

Was it the part when I brought tears to your eyes for the same reason I brought a smile to your face and glitter to your cheeks slightly brushed on blush, oh what a rush when you touch me back for the way I've been touching you...

Was it the part when we stayed up a quarter pass dark and 7 minutes into twilight being extra tender with each other, pillow talking in sheets of seduction under sinless covers that exposed our naked truths and the secrets I shared with only you...

Was it the part when I held your hand and pulled you close gave you my coat on that night stroll for the comfort of security and my good council to help you find the answer within yourself because I was only thinking of
you...

Was it the part when I wrote this poem with no ink or paper, no pride or prejudice , no shit and no joke , no way I can be this open and watch you shut the door, you're going to have to come outside so I can tell you again, Why
I LOVE YOU...

99 ATTRIBUTES

* Kisses Kill *

I ain't never had a home ,
and half of the kisses today ain't worth the
spit that lick'um wet, I'm so miserably happy
in my loneliness , that I just gotta reach out
to be touched and since you left your
fingerprints on me,
you owe me that
Much...

Like high school crushes that fukc up your
grades..
I kinda asked for this shit and if you don't
like the smell, then plug your nose and
whisper my name, its still going to turn out
the same, and if you back me into a corner,
I'm'a blame it on the Boogie...
I did that for a
Touch...

I'm not guilty
if thighs keep their legs closed, but i'm like
that Fiona Apple type of criminal , what I
need is a good defense, a Hung jury from the
sheets that held her hostage , she left her
orgasm for evidence,
Exhibit#
Soul Spill...

99 ATTRIBUTES

I wiped my mouth clean of these kisses, but heartbreak diaries never let the ink dry..
So you still want to hurt me with your love huh? Well go ahead, I been shot before,..
But never through the heart like this, every tear goin' cry its own tears, you can't just run out in these roses ..
Because
Kisses
Kill...

99 ATTRIBUTES

* Shug Avery's Courage *

She's choking my Love...
Like hold up... Y'all Muthafukcas just gonna stand there,
Like I ain't meant shit to you,
I done put my Heart under Abrahams Knife on a Cold slab of Sacrifice , and shot Dice with Malcolm X rifle to kill all my Chances of ever finding innocence in lies that ring True....
I've ran Lips over Hot Passion Coals and Blistered Kisses for staring me Down, as if you know something about this Bowlegged Piano Song,
I've Cultured Women in the Fine Art of Moaning and Silly Syllables and Sonnet Shorthands with Soul Soaked Signature Smiles, She ain't never felt that Weak going Strong....
Don't talk to me about Love,
I have defeated every would be, wannabe, really now, you really think you got what it takes, to take me there ,
I've burnt bridges to stand alone on a heap of broken hearts and souls,
Cliffhanging from a
Dead End
Road,
I've nursed a Rose in the Freezing Cold, watched her Shiver and Shake, Begging me

99 ATTRIBUTES

not to leave her Alone in this icicle hold
with Chilled Daggers, I staggered,
Bleeding to take her
Home ....
Looking Love in the Eyes ,
I Linger Lost in a Lounging Lullaby to Lure
her Legs Longitude and mangle her hips
Loose in Licks of Lust, she Lays in   wait of
me
In
Laughs,
And y'all got a Front Row Seat, with The
Loudest Hecklers   Talking all through my
shit,
Like Look, this is the Part like Shug's
Redemption Song, where He gets to Save
His own
Azz...

99 ATTRIBUTES

* Everyday Love *

Good Morning Love, you're like a purple dawn on the cusp of a ruby red sunrise, with orange tint and honey yellow lip gloss shining your smile across my horizon , I'm sleep walking in your dreams over the waters of your Soul...

I want this Time,.. Everyday Love..

Good Afternoon Love, you're like Gold glitter wrapped in blues, under a sweat dripping sky, with passion in the air setting our tongues on fire trying to have a conversation over a sidewalk lunch with two orders of ice water to boil and steam our Kisses...

I want this time, Everyday Love...

Good Night Love, you're like a blushing Moon illuminating my darkest nights, with a lullaby between your thighs and the   stars dancing on your shoulders, dipped in chocolate shadows and soothing whispers

99 ATTRIBUTES

that curl your eyelashes as we melt our lips
into a sweet
Rest...

I want this time, Everyday Love...

99 ATTRIBUTES

* THIS *

You always Tempting me,
and Tampering with my Touch,
Tugging on my Tongue and Talking like you Taste,
Tenderoni on Tantalizing Thighs,
Peppered and Seasoned, Turn you over on your Tummy and poke a Tickle, Through your Throat and bite Through This Talk,
you got me Tanqueray Tipsy and Tripping over my Today, Tonight and Tomorrow,
I Tear The Truth out of secrets and Tell Tall Tales that bottom out of the
Top,
Then cut the sky open with my falcon wing Tip,
and watch Topaz Blue Tumble down like the slow melt of
chocolate Turtles ,
let's Toss it up like Tupac,
and Turn it up like gossip Talk,
like who you
Telling..
Twirling Tinsels with
Textbook
Testimonies ,
and to Think,
I Trusted you,
but you were just
Teasing all This

99 ATTRIBUTES

Time,
playing your Tambourine on my
Tangible
Thoughts,
you must be some type of magic Trick,
black smoke Transfixed ,
like me Trying To write
THIS...

99 ATTRIBUTES

* CLICK *

Look, I know we're married and all, but I was thinking maybe I could steal you from me for the night, I know this fly little jazz spot just off Crenshaw next to the Fish Fry, about 3 blocks away from your Momma's house, you know that joint with the blues lights where the spoken word Poets leave spit on the Mic,
Don't worry about what to wear , I picked you out something that matches perfectly with that Beautiful Smile of yours, and you know me being your Man, I can come through the door any second , so get dressed before I catch me sneaking you out, and sock me in the mouth, like she ain't leaving this house without her wedding Ring, and I like how you move that thing, when I'm trying to make eye contact , you pinball me down your curves, like turn around let me see why your husband is so jealous , but im'a secure that tonight until you take bites out of your bottom lip and offer me the Biggest Slice,
Oh don't worry about me, we'll be long gone before I get home, now you just relax yourself and let's braid our fingers together, is that the perfume I bought you? I bet I ain't never smelled it like this before, sweet

99 ATTRIBUTES

scented neckline just begging for cinnamon
toasted hickies, we may never make it to the
show, the way you look under that cherry
moon, dancing in your hair with tangled
stars and glitter on your shoulders, your
husband ain't never seen you with these eyes,
so let me close yours under licks and moans,
and Uh, turn off your phone because I know
I'm'a be blowing you up, like where you at
and who you with.. And I know you don't
wanna hear that tonight.. So
CLICK...

99 ATTRIBUTES

* Paper Rose *

I meet a Poem today,
Who told me Her name was Poetry,
I introduced myself as Poet and wrote it
Over the horizon,
so
She wouldn't miss it at the end of my
Page...

She had cried Herself blurred lines with so
many commas, it was commonplace to find
her on the verb of run on sentences and
abstract conclusions, that grease the mouth
for tongue
Braids...

She was Write after all, Love is Paper Thin,
See Through and Easy to Tear and She had
the ripped edges to prove her point beyond
the shadow of a
Period...

She was Cute, Curious, Conflicted,
Conscious, Careless , Cautious , Cultured,
Clingy, Clumsy , Choosy, Cheesy, Childish ,
Chatty, Centered, Covert,
Claudine, Come Close, Cashmere,
Cursory, Clandestine, So Cool and Dead
Bang
Serious...

99 ATTRIBUTES

It was Written all over her Face, I was Proof Reading into her Prose, into her Closet with her Clothes, into her Business that was Closed, but She opened her Eyes and let me into her
Soul...

I'm trying to squeeze my grammar into her College Rule, I'm a Fumbling Fool, She said Word?... So you never finished school ? Naw I dropped out to Finish You, like Adult Classes at Night, between your Smile and The Moon,
And I'm Plucking that She Loves Me and Loves Me Not
On a
Paper
Rose...

99 ATTRIBUTES

* LOVE NOTES #86 *

This is no way to Kill a Poet,
She didn't even let the Ink Dry
Before She Crumbled me up
and tossed me into the
Furnace,...
I mean I thought we were better
than Words, with Matching Hearts
In Him & Hers, and Exclusively
Preferred like a One Time Only
Purchase,...
Silly of Me and Deniece Williams
For thinking I could Survive Her
Kisses when She Couldn't Care
Less, The Mourning of a Love
Letter to a Woman I even Loved
In The
Third
Person...

* Kisses & Huggs # 18 *

She got the kind of loving that can hurt between kisses,
placing my Big pillowed lips
in-between her sleeping thighs to squeeze my kisses for comfort because its so agonizing not to feel her skin between my dreams,
on hourglass beach sand counting forever til we can touch secrets,
and her hips go so good with mine, grinding our bones into sugar spills,
Here...
Put this on your tongue and tell me what I taste like between Moans...

99 ATTRIBUTES

* I'm Just Saying # 25 *

The Top of the World is the Bottom of Hell,
I caught the Devil by the Tail, but Broke My Pinky Nail,
I'm in Love with Kushite Women who speak Arabic Blowing me Kisses from Behind the Veil,
I'm like a Slave on Sale, I'm a Bargain for Housewives who need a story to Tell.
I got a story to Yell, from the Roof of my Mouth, my Tonsils are like ringing Bells,
Just like the Call to Prayer, I gotta Beg for Mercy, I picked up my Blessings where My Knees Fell,
I Heard Life Stinks, So I Wear Egyptian Musk just to hide the Smell,
I meet my Wife Online, I was Zapp'd by Computer Love, but if She ever leave me I'm Hooking Up with Dell,
I'm too Young to be this Grey, and too Old to be going to Jail,

99 ATTRIBUTES

Every Decision I make is Life and Death,
They won't sit me in a Box to go Stale,
I'm in the Prison of my Passions having an Intellectual Breakthrough,...Like Duh... I got Poetry to Sell
Send me to Mecca and I'll come back an Imam with a Sermon to Preach, titled , " The Top of The World is The Bottom of Hell "...

99 ATTRIBUTES

* A Quickie # 23 *

She was cute around the edges where
most beautiful things lack in contrast,
had a softness that rivaled cotton
candy and clouded dreams,
I was crushing with a touch-less feel
that felt fond of the fact I couldn't
fathom or fancy my defenseless foolish
fumble of words like powdered sugar
on funnel cake I was falling flat on my
face in front of her fragrance
trying to say something
Fresh...

* Love Notes # 11 *

How many times have I chased love phantoms into the shadows of broken lamps
Grasping at words that dissolve like sugar cubes on watered tongues...
I'm an Oasis for broken-hearts, fallen tears and scorned women, they use my beaches to wash away their sorrows on the dreams of my tomorrow's while basking in
My
Sun....
I'm the only lonely between kissing lips that never meet at the anniversary of my smile twirling by myself on the crowded dance floor of flatfooted
Passion....
They throw red wine roses at my feet, making me slip and fall into the laps of laughing women who lunge at my heart like free shoes and purses and I can't
Stop
Them
From
Grabbing,...
Like prison yard stabbings, I'm left to choke on my own love,
Spilling out soul confessions trying to stomach butterflies
on the belly of caterpillars breathing my

99 ATTRIBUTES

Last
Whisper,..
I'm a crumbled poem in a rained on parade,
watch me bleed my ink in the streets and
flood Lovers Lane, so enjoy the swim before
you pull my drain ,
with my last
Drip
I
Kissed
Her...

99 ATTRIBUTES

* Kisses & Huggs #13 *

Home-cooked Love will make a vegan fat, medicine, faith and prayer, the Prefect One and the Pair, Three slices of Pizza's can feed an Army, we can go belly up with this and love with an Appetite, you can be purified by sin or corrupted by holiness , im'a swing between your thighs on a passion summer's fly over your peaks and valley lows, your middle earth swim, where we all emerge from the deep, just let me Love you , from your melt down to your
Feet...

99 ATTRIBUTES

* I'm Just Saying # 75 *

I got Trust issues,
I don't Trust Tissue,
To Hold my Tears,
Or Mask my Fears,
I'm Loyal to a Fault,
But here's a Thought,
is it Cheating to Talk,
I'm Caught in a Catch 22
With 21 Questions, so this ONE's here for You,
Do you want to Ruin my Good Name,
I mean I got a different feel
but I hurt just the Same,
I'll burn the Blues,
I'm like that Purple Rain Dude,
You Fukcin' with Morris?,
I'll Slap Apollonia too!!!
Jealous!!???... You damn right,
I don't deny what's True,
Like Religious Jeans, I even bought a pair for you,
But a Woman look more Woman in a Dress,
I got Old World Values,
Talking New School Fresh,
I don't Play with God, but He got some Jokes for Me,
So I'm laughing at my Life,

99 ATTRIBUTES

because He's The Most to
Me,
Don't get Too Close Me, I'm known to
Handcuff the
Innocent,
Me and My Prison Mentality,
I'm giving out Life
Sentences,
Imagine That, better yet I like to Imagine
Blacks,
Ruling Europeans like the Moors, Lets bring
them
Classics Back,
But I was shoot in the Mouth for talking like
That,
I'm on my El Hajj Malik El Shabazz, I'll be
killed by Government Backed
Blacks,
And The White Girl said I Love your
Message what can I do to Help,
NOTHING!!!! We gotta do this Ourselves,
Oh, and before y'all knock me off of my
Soapbox,
Bismillah Ar-Rahman Ar-Raheem...
Now take your Best
Shot!!!...

* A Quickie # 14 *

Something of her kiss remained on my lips long after her spit had dried as lip balm fermentation of intoxicating love and I still carry her lipstick runoff inside the cracks of my lips, like paper bag spirits, and now you know why I'm so drunk on
Love...

99 ATTRIBUTES

* Laughs Above a Smile *

She had a Laugh that was Kisses
Above any pair of Lips tickled by
A Smile,
A Beauty that was Broken into Dawns and
Sunsets with Swan littered Ponds,
Like we should stay here for
Awhile,
Rolling Hills with Pearl Blue Skies,
She had thunder in her Hips and Rain
in her Thighs, Soul full of Silk and Teeth
Full of
Milk,
Poured me a Glass and We Rolled in the
Grass, reached for the Stars and Spilled
Out of our Jars, We left Wet on the
Quilt,
She had the Faith of Maryam and The
Features of Aishah wrapped in Earth linens
I called her Chocolate Yemen and She was
Just as Kush as all
Arabian Women,
She had a Laugh that was Kisses
Above any pair of Lips tickled by
A Smile,
I told her Sister Khadijah, I haven't seen her
since Medinah, She said you can find her
Giggling on the Banks of
The Blue Nile...

99 ATTRIBUTES

* Bleeding Ink *

My Poem is a jealous Woman,
And I Love her to The End of every Word,
I Love to Pen her Down between these Sheets,
And ask Her, where you think you're going Dressed like that...
She says " Oh My Jealous Poet".... Find me a Book Cover and Secure your Lover...
I don't want nobody to read Her but Me...
And She doesn't want nobody to Write Her but
Me...
So I've been sneaking Love Notes in between her pages...
She said its like me placing my tongue between her thighs,
She had to lick my fingers just to turn the Page....
And I'm still stuck on our last words... That brought her to her Period...
She said not tonight darling....
But don't let me find you penning other Poems...
I swear I'll rip every page out of her ass to pieces...
Now y'all see why I Love Her to Pieces,

99 ATTRIBUTES

I've been writing her Pieces as My Thesis....
But I can't write shit til this
Ink stop
Bleeding...

99 ATTRIBUTES

* Love Notes # 101 *

Me and my Big Mouth Soul, I'm always
spilling my guts because I have a heart that
likes to stand naked on
A Soapbox,
Aim and shoot your arrows I dare you, I
won't even protect myself from you, I'm that
bold and tender and I'll show you how a
Mans tears
Drop,
With the weight of heaven,
I'll crush all your preconceived ideas of me
and take you behind the veil,
But you gotta come naked , leave your purse
and heels behind and throw your panties to
the wind, because I'm going to show you
what
I can't
Tell...

You can only skinny-dip with me, nothing
can stand between us, not even air, we
breathe each other for
Life,
So when you finish undressing
Let's smash these mirrors and amalgamate
through a kiss so you can see what I'm really
Like just before

99 ATTRIBUTES

I
Husband
Your
Wife...

* Kisses & Huggs # 39 *

She tied my kisses in a knot and held me to a compromise between heart and soul, I'm a hostage she can't let go, She gave me her word as I was massaging the skin of her teeth because she said the sweetest things, like if birds don't teach bees how to fly sweetness will never reach your lips under honey rich skies, She likes to riddle her ripples through my passion like that, and I don't mind because she squeeze those thighs around my neck and get me all choked up like Muslim bow-ties ain't that the Truth, like preaching poetry from the pulpit with one congregational member seeking a testimony and a confession that could only Render me guilty, praying 5 times a day, and she still finds room for me to Sin, like a Saint,
He
Ain't...

99 ATTRIBUTES

* I'm Just Saying # 12 *

I'm a Dying Breed,
I'm the Root of Adams Apple Seed...
I'm cut from Kente Cloth...
I'm too Chicken to go Vegan, but I'm so Close, I could just taste it like Vegetable Broth...
I'm Broken in 7 Pieces, pulled apart by Nephews and Nieces, and it's much more Harder to say No to Daughters,
But I'm a Step Up Father so they Kill me with Love, like I'm an Old Tender Hearted Monster...
I Barter with Death like I Owe Life and I just pawned my Last Breath, Had to Borrow an Exhale from my Wife wishing I could pay her back with a Baby Chugging Her Womb Water....
I'm as Tempted as Christ, 40 Days and 40 Nights, 40 Pokes and 40 Likes , I'm 41 , so I made it Right?... She like Naw, you owe me One for that Shit you Write....

99 ATTRIBUTES

I'm Fasting Furious like 12 Months of Ramadan,
I'm like a Meeting of The Minds, between The Imam and Farrakhan,
With all my Faith, Fornication and Forgiveness , I'm
Fresh out Frying Pan and it was Hotter than Fish Grease ,
Oh Hell, I'm on Ether Fire,
And Some Sister with a Blunt had the nerves to ask me for a Light ...

* A Quickie # 53 *

I want your morning
Over Easy
Your Moon running
Creamy
Your Thighs Yawning with The
dawning of Bedroom Eyes and your
Skin spilling over into
Dreamy,
Slumped in your Breath with your
Belly laying
Sleepy,
I want you to stay just like that
Like Henna
Never
Leave
Me...

99 ATTRIBUTES

Deeper Heights
by Kimathi El Shabazz collab w SunshineIs Ayana

Kimathi~ Care to take a dive with me
into deeper skies
with a breathless whisper held between
thighs
under a moonlit kiss into the heart of
Heavens
Secret...

SunshineIs~ I will follow you
wherever you lead
taking me to the place in your mind
that keeps me satisfied
intertwined in a slow wine
as the stars beam upon us
swaying back & forth to the sweet
melody of our song
It wont be long

Kimathi~ Barefoot souls gracing life's
dance floor to the
music of songbirds as I reach for your
hand

99 ATTRIBUTES

across the sands of time
swimming in ocean filled tears that
wash me
up onto the beaches of your tropical
smile
you're like a mouthful of sweet
Summer
Peaches...

SunshineIs~ Kissing my heart ever so
soft
taking away the pain of all the love
lost
you touch my soul in ways unknown
as you water my rose
my petals have grown
the colors are bright
what a lovely sight

Kimathi~ Lets keep air under our feet
& run our toes
through the clouds, fill our wounds
with kisses
& rescue our dreams from the pillows
that
cried us to sleep with a
Lonely

99 ATTRIBUTES

Lullaby...

SunshineIs~ If you let me go I will surely fall
tired of the nightmares that just wont stall
ready to envision the fantasies
that flow free between you & me
lets become 1 & forever be WE

Kimathi~ I wanna be your Good Morning sunrise who
you kept up all night dancing in your moonlight, falling upwards with the sky
under our wings as we splash in each others
Eyes...

SunshineIs~ I'll be your goodnight
waking with you in the morning light
soaring like eagles
shining as diamonds
Are you ready to fly...

By WE

99 ATTRIBUTES

* While I Wonder *

He may wonder what you look like...?

While I wonder what you think like, how you breathe life, do you scream wife, do you lean right, and are you mean on them greens and those red beans & rice....

He may wonder how big your booty is...?

While I wonder how deep your beauty is, do you swim in soul, light and love, take to the sky and dance on wind, tickle happiness with your smile at the point of joy where your lips bend...

He may wonder are you a freak in bed...?

While I wonder are you sweet instead and what your teachers said, do you pray before bed and what's the last book you read, do you kiss with your heart and laugh in your head, do you mourn for the living and smile for the dead and how many children do you want to share our slice of bread....

He may wonder do you cover like that out of fear and oppression...?

99 ATTRIBUTES

While I wonder will you cover my flaws
with faith and blessings, will you map out
the garden of bliss with your hands of henna
and protect what's precious, do you read The
Quran and live its lessons , do you fight for
justice, peace and
breakfast,
so we can feed the hungry ,
donate to poor women your
dresses and spread love as your living
message...

He may wonder how tasty your flesh is...?

While I wonder beneath your skin that I may
taste your essence...

99 ATTRIBUTES

* Pieces *

Her lips had loaded kisses and pieces of a
man that he couldn't get back,
she was a smile covered heartbreak just
waiting to happen and I so happened to trip
over her beauty which I found painfully
similar to mine, only she gave it dimpled
cuteness with a sweeter sound that was
music to my Song...

We were like kissing cousins, she was so
strangely familiar , like we did this before,
in a different life time ,
in different bodies,
on different soil ,
for the same reasons,
with the same kisses,
under the same blushes, rushing in like
fools,
with that down home feeling of deep soul
blues,
felt like tasting the sky with dreamy eyes,
gazing over pools of cool, traveling on light
and our kisses made time
Pause ...

We had an unfinished type of love ,
like there was always something else to it...

99 ATTRIBUTES

maybe I was guilty of loving on an empty
stomach and bit off more than I could chew,
kissing with my mouth full, where's my
manners...
Would you like
A Piece?

99 ATTRIBUTES

* Don't ask me about Love *

Don't ask me about Love, because I'll set butterflies on fire, make doves cry and put dimples in the smiles of lady bugs...
Dance on the crystal lakes of your eyes, swim in the buttercream of your thighs, jump off a waterfall and splash into the sky, candy necklace lip bites and tummy to tummy full belly Huggs...
I'm the longing that travels up the curves of your legs like black lace thigh-highs reaching for your hips, as my tongue leaps out of my mouth only to be caught between your knees ....
Squeeze and feel me burst this love nectar til I saturate your petals in Heart pulp, stuck all between your teeth, try sucking me out with your tongue and I won't even let you breathe...
Don't ask me about Love because I'll play the saxophone on your collarbone , uncross your legs and make ballads spill romantic symphonies , I got
Enough gospel to rhythm your Blues..
I'm like your new purse and shoes you just gotta show me off and wrap me around your finger like a bloodless diamond wedding ring, because if you don't look good, I don't

99 ATTRIBUTES

look good... I'm lying cause I'm'a still look good but not nearly as good as I would With You....
I'll dive into your bellybutton to womb swim in the depths of your soul where the hands of God fashions babies out of tears and love, heartbreak and promise , pain and laughter and every contradiction held between a Kiss...
Don't ask me about Love, because I've given sacrifice known to nail a prophet to wood and prostitute for baby diapers and milk, you can't break my heart enough so why not love me and put a smile on your face and let me show you how to treat your Lips...
Just don't ask me about Love...when I've already answered your Heart...

99 ATTRIBUTES

* HOOK or CROOK # 8 *

Don't be with me for Poetry
I'll Drive a Woman up the Wall
and
Over The Rainbow,
Like is She Happy or Gay,
Who can Say in this modern
Day,
I could be wrong in everything I'm doing
Write,
Just ask my Wife,
She takes the Biggest Bite.
Nibble through my Notebook,
Like Nooks and Cranberry
Juice,
Dip your Lips in Ink and Tongue Kiss my
Poetry,
I'm
As Kick Ass
As
Bruce,
With Termite insecurities that chew through
my Hardwood floors,
Watch where you step, you could fall
through and land in my basement belly up
into my torture chambers,
I'm a Stranger to Myself,
A Danger to everybody Else,
The only time I was Balling is when Ni##as
were wearing

99 ATTRIBUTES

Pagers,
Now I'm as Broke as Hearts,
With a Family Bigger than my Wallet,
Y'all had Steak and Lobster for Dinner,
and all I had was a
Whatchamacallit,
They telling me to go Hustle Poetry,
Get your Paper Up by
Selling Books,
HOOK or CROOK...

99 ATTRIBUTES

* What That Mean ? *

She stay in the hood like Trayvon with a bag
of skittles , a little too cute for these streets
but don't let that fool you,
Her Father is an old time hustler turned
Muslim and her Momma use to bake bean
pies in Philly, back when The Imam was just
a young man trying to grasp Allah's plan...
She was raised under good teachings ,
like on Good Times when James put up a
picture of Black Jesus,
it was all Love and steamed vegetables ,
family prayers and study hour, She was
flowered in the right soil ,
never thought almond milk could spoil, but
these streets will test your Deen ,
your troubles don't end on the prayer rug,
that's where they begin for men, women and
jinn, smoking that hookah and Philly blunts ,
trying to understand the lay of the land, the
gun in the hand and the animal in man,
She was caught in a cold blizzard   with
snakes, frogs, dogs and lizards , chicken shit
niggas who ain't worth their own gizzards...
She got her heart broke with a full belly, and
y'all wonder why these children are
heartless,
don't be the cutest be the smartest,

99 ATTRIBUTES

don't be drawn in by a bullshit artist who can't draw a straight line with his crooked eyes and twisted mind,
trying to pretzels your thighs and give you more than enough reasons to cry,
The Good Lord gave you common sense, don't get wet by that spit and slip on that nickel slick talk, Atomic Dog, why must he chase the Kat,
can't keep him on your lap , he out there setting rat traps..save the applause , he done brought home the Clap...
Small time jive ass, nickel and dime ass, only read The Quran when he's on the prison yard,
but you done with him putting his hands on you.. Them letters are returned back to sender,
She had to find her inner worth and work that Faith on her off days,
had to barter her EBT card for a few dollars so she could pay her way up to the community college,
go in-search of that knowledge
like every Prophet to Muhammad, She need higher degrees to get out of that deep freeze,
early morning Quranic studies with prayers spilling over her knees,
She's back on her Deen,
Black flag over her face..
what'cha think that Mean?

99 ATTRIBUTES

* IF I DIE TONIGHT *
(Remix / If I Die Tonight by Tupac Shakur)

They Say Pu$$y and Paper is Poetry,
Power and Pistols;
Plotting to Purge in Purgatory while
Taking Pictures,
Pissing on Pitiful Punk Persians begging
Please,
With Prayer Beads as I Position myself on
Fajr Knees,
My enemies blabber in suicidal
conversations,
Never to Witness, like my Shahada,
Declaration,
Masjids are Packed, with Residents,
Perfume and
Incense,
Evading the Prayer Hating Women,
Who don't
Listen,
B!tches will bad mouth, I'm Prayer calling in
my Thobe,
And y'all been Told,
No QURAN should be
Sold,
I'm sick of The Profit Society,
Allah Save Me,
Addicted to Rakus, and No,..My Mama
didn't

99 ATTRIBUTES

Name Me,
Even The Imam and all my Teachers still
Greet Me,
I Return it with Peace, while Puffing
Hookah with My Peeps,
I'm ducking the Cop, I grab my prayer beads
as I'm clutching my
Glock,
MUSLIMS do Not wanna miss Salat,
What IF I DIE TONIGHT...

Power to The People, Prepare for Battle Pass
The Pump,
See I'm with The Prophet(pbuh),
Devils is dropping then they
Done,
Calling The Adhan, Come Collect The Zakat
but of course ,
He got it by The Pillar, Preoccupied with
Righteous Thoughts,
Islam is The Message, No Overstepping,
Keep your Ears
Close,
Adversaries are Overdosed on My Poetic
Notes,
Jealous Devils and THOT b!tches equal
Packed Jails,
Make Salat, Heal your Soul, they're killing
Black Males,

99 ATTRIBUTES

Picture Perfection, Pursuing Paradise with a Passion,
Religion in Prison with no Pu$$y but I'm Lasting,
Running with Principled Individuals and What's Important,
Don't Try to Stop Me, My Muslim Army, Using Righteous Force,
In My Brain all I can Think about is 99 Names,
The Police know my Face, a Different Day, ain't a Thing Changed,
I'm seeing Cemetery Photos of my Beard,
Combing through my Chin, like I'm still Here,...
IF I DIE TONIGHT...

Pu$$y and Paper is Poetry,
Power and Pistols;
Plotting to Purge in Purgatory while Taking Pictures,
Pray to The Heavens, QURAN Three: Fifty Seven to The Sky,
And I hope I'm Forgiven for Cuzz Crippin' when I Die,
I wonder if Heaven will Unite Me with Blood Niggaz,

99 ATTRIBUTES

A Stress Free Life and a Spot for Drug Dealers,
Cotton Picking while Practicing how to Pimp The System, Playa,
Overstanding my d!ck, Stopped Drinking Liquor for My Prayers,
Pickle Dipping These Chics, with Pedicures and Fresh Braids,
I'm Retrospecting The Game,
Praying for Punishment and Pain to go Away,
Going Insane, Never Die, Live Eternal, Who Shall I Fear?
Don't shed a Tear for Me Ahk,
I ain't Happy
Here,
I hope they Bury me and send me to my Rest,
Headlines reading ... MUSLIM IN DEATH,
My Last Breath,
Take a Look, Got My Book in my Right Hand,
Men, Women and Jinn, Don't Understand,
IF I DIE TONIGHT...

99 ATTRIBUTES

* Black Woman *

I seen a Sister so Coal Black, it was as if I seen Eve herself, She said she's from Yemen, Arabia, Nubia, Kushite Woman if you must,
She was craved out of her own mind, the scales of justice were on her shoulders and she breathed   life into ashes and
dust,
She put Heaven on her smile and gave birth to the universe and she said earth is her
Garden,
I asked if I could walk with her so I could further talk with her, she agreed and I stepped into her
Darkness,
With a light so bright it blew the Skin right off of my
Soul,
and I bathed like new life, it was like swimming in liquid
Gold,
She grieved for earthlings and created oceans from her
Tears,
She snapped me with her heart and I just spilled all over her
Cheer,
Her happiness and Joy was blissfully
Divine,

99 ATTRIBUTES

I'm like a grape on her vine and she squeeze life from between her thighs,
Popped into the world from this sweet black Girl, Woman and Goddess and I'm still being modest,
She danced inside my eyes, and weeped with my cries , and she told me the truth so we could talk honest,
She said The Children of the Sun should rest in her Moonlight on Love pillows birthing stars into The Universe,
Take good care of the Earth, stop spilling blood, for I have already fulfilled her Thirst,
Dance at your work, and laugh with your tears,
You die when you fear, and all your answers are between your ears,
But give it to your hearts and let it refine your divine ,
You're precious in my eyes, and you can stay between my thighs, so we could multiply, add on and divide , the common denominator and The Square root of One,
The Kiss on the Soul and the soft blush of Love,
Remember your Youth and stay as deep as your roots,
You can die in a lie or live in the truth,
Husband your wives, and wives be brides,
Light up his skies, and share with him your Divine,

99 ATTRIBUTES

Man be a Man, provide and protect , love with valor ,
Help cultivate her garden and offer her it's flowers,
Let children's laughter tickle your womb,
Be as puddin on a spoon, just as yummie in your tummie ,
But then I asked her,..do you love me?, then she hugged me, I love you like you love me, with a big jar of honey,
In-between these waking dreams and falling back in love again,
Your rich dark chocolate black skin,
A friend to the Sun, protected under love,
I'm tangled in her hair, tied with ropes like vines on trees,
Just as natural as you ought to be,
Your rhythm your style , those dimples those smiles those stars in the corners of your eyes, gazing through life as the pleasure to be Free,
Kiss me into illumination til I float and pop my balloon against your crispy blue skies I jumped up out into my Soul and took a cosmic dive,
My kisses on her lips ran straight to her thighs, I stopped it at her knees, and licked it up her spine ,
She giggled at her neck, and I tickled down her sweat, we wet like chocolate pools, drenched in pheromones ,

99 ATTRIBUTES

And loving in the cool, refreshed and brand new, our souls are in the nude,, I'm her, she's me, we're one that split as two,
Like taffy tugs and Elmer's glue, I'm stuck to her like what wouldn't I do ?
I put a swans pond on her belly so she could feel me, fly, fall and dive dead smack into her jelly,
I remember your dance across the sands of time, the daughters of Ethiopia , the Queens of Kemet, The Kushite blood line the original and divine
The drum beat of her people , played on the hearts of those who dared to love,
I can't stop kissing and hugging , falling back in loving, dancing into the twilight into the kisses of the sky,...I call her black berry pie, and you call her Black Woman!!!

99 ATTRIBUTES

* Just After Dark *

I would love to dance with you on the bright
side of a Nubian moon under a crisp
midnight Afrikan sky,
With a Mali drum beat vibe groovin' through
your thighs, filling up your soul and spilling
out of your eyes,
Joyful tears bring rain which springs a
garden oasis out of Sahara sand,
As we ride on the backs of the Lions of
Tanzania across the stretch of the land,
Seeding the Earth with Love and Flowers ,
under the showers of Blessings and Big Lip
kisses while holding
Hands,
Diving into the Nile from the peaks of the
pyramids as I swim across your smile only
to drown in our Forever Right Now,
Into a blood orange evening sky, tasting
citrus flavored air while catching butterflies
in your hair,
At the Zambezi river drinking from the
waterfalls of Mosi-oa-Tunya, with your
candy yam sweetness and the hips of a pear ,
You've been dipped in the Sun like black
gold radiating creaminess, like sunbathing in
Shea Butter,
As you color summer with
beauty and wonder, under the clouds of
Kush, we recline into the comfort of lovers,

99 ATTRIBUTES

While my kisses on the back of your neck
drip into puddles at the small of back,
Like chocolate prayer beads melting over
your curves ,
Lord have mercy, I'll eat watermelon out of
your
Lap,
Until you sugarcoat my lips in the honey
flow of your blackberry pie,
If I'm sinning , I've been forgiven by the
Women of Yemen who told me that Lovers
are their own Mecca, so make a   pilgrimage
to your own heart, and I blew the Moon out,
Just After
Dark...

99 ATTRIBUTES

* Colorful *

She was Yellow Black, As Dark as The Sun
On a Golden Night,
YellowBone under Buttered Skin, losing herself in fields of daffodils, basking in Sunflower Light,
I was Her Dark Chocolate Craving, Bathing in Arabian Nights, A BlueBone, I make Teeth look even more White, My Smile Shines even more Bright, My Touch feels even more Right, The Blackest Berry is ever so
Ripe,
So I made her my Wife, So we could Make Sugar Babies, you know the Cute little Brown type, I had'um doing Somersaults in her Belly, like Happy Kushites,
As She just Smiled and Said,
I Just Love Our Colorful
Life...

99 ATTRIBUTES

* OverSlept *

She taught me how to Dream in
Peppermint ,
Soul Scented Silk Runoff, and Yemen
Merchant
Frankincense,
Sand Sandals and Camel Rides across a
Krinkled Kushite Burgundy Sky,
Like a Thousand Arabian Midnights,
Her Lips Stained in
Poet's Ink,
Shadow Slivers
and Broken
Moonlight ,
She waited 999 Years,
went to Methuselah's
Wake,
While I OverSlept in Rhythm Folds, Time
Lapse over Lap Time, Sleepy Thighs, I
couldn't catch up Where Time
Ran
Late,
But I seen it on Her Face,
Like a Dream that Lose Count,
She Caught Up with
Forever,
And Said,
Don't let your Dreams
Steal your Now,
I was too Patient to interrupt

99 ATTRIBUTES

a Dream Love,
Young Girls wait for
Never,
But Old Women
Know
Better,
She taught me how to Dream in the
Foolishness of
Youth,
and
I woke up Grey,
Bent over Looking
For the Things
We Meant
To
Do...

99 ATTRIBUTES

* Broke Wing Walk *

He got a Girlfriend and a Wife on the
Side,
And She don't gotta Pretend they're just
Friends
They're just stealing
Time,
They Done Crossed The Line and Crossed
Their
Hearts,
He Crossing his fingers, that She
Uncross her Legs,
Unbutton his Hands and Undo her
Hair,
Keeping the Sun
in the
Dark,...
Guilty Pleasures
and
Filthy Feathers,
Fallen Angels
and
They know
Better,
These Bowlegged Blues, Bend and Break
Fools, Bogus Blush, is Blemish and Blotch,
These Weights
and
Measures,
He can't Stay, Duty and Obligation and

99 ATTRIBUTES

Love Should've
Brought his
Azz
Home ...
She got up under his Skin and put
Goosebumps on his
Bones ,
But they walk a Crooked Line,
Sneaking up
to
a
Kiss
on their
Tippy
Toes...
He pulls away,
His Wife can taste lipstick on his Thoughts
and
The Breath of a
Woman's
Talk,
She said it ain't
No Love
Lost,
It's just a
Broke
Wing
Walk....

99 ATTRIBUTES

* NICE TRY *

Here's a heartbreak story that'll bottom out tear ducts,
rip the wings off of butterflies and spill the glitter of slaughtered
unicorns,
bleed the color out of roses,
and kiss the Moon Goodbye...

They had a Love story torn from the pages of fairy tales , Love at first sight will make a blind date see the Sun and Moon sneak away behind clouds to frolic in the sky in full view of Lovers gazing with warm smiles spilling over their chins and splashing into their
Thighs...

They were too good to be true
like twin souls
with matching socks and
kisses never tasted so hot,
burnt their tongues to ashes with a flaming passion that was cozy like campfire blanket cuddles under a Dark Chocolate
Sky...

99 ATTRIBUTES

But they didn't see the storm coming too
busy dreaming, sleep walking and sweet
talking,
like happiness is debt free ,
every smile is paid for with tears and they
bought love on credit with a penny less than
a dime and collections is always on
Time...

They fell from the stars and belly flopped on
that old wasteland of heartbreak where the
broken pieces of love are still sharp enough
to impale the most tender of kisses
and best of intentions ,
best of wishes to the broken collarbones that
use to moan under lip tugs with quivers that
milk the
Spine...

They became stale like duck bread,
couldn't understand the silence that was once
songs of
jubilee ,
like holding hands with sand,
they just couldn't hold it together, they were
too delicate for this love that swings down
like a sledgehammer,
this is a battlefield where dreamers are
violently awaken and taken from their sweet
lullabies ,

99 ATTRIBUTES

you gotta knuckle up for wedding rings,
don't lose your knees,
this is where hearts fight like gladiators for
one last dream ...
they weren't ready for this...
But
Nice
Try...

* Poet's Rehab *

What better way to exit the stage, than to remember the poems that got me here, the emotions that I've exploited as therapeutic healing, the killings that occurred that left ink spillings all over the paper floors of the world....
I never asked for this, a broken heart, a concubine and marriage did this to me, I've only been writing the same poem over and over again because nobody seems to understand that I got ink for tears, my love fights my fears, my faith has outgrown my beard and my own family think I'm weird...
Pain inspires me, Beauty ignites me, Women entice me and invite me to places I can't go,
Men give me 5 on the Black hand side and Salute me, and I bow with humility, I'm humble to the bone, but I couldn't read every poem and poets are so sensitive that we scream for attention... Somebody Read Me..., Somebody Listen to Me.... Pleasssse... I Swear I'll be honest, deep and

intriguing.... I just don't want y'all to ignore me....

I feel like an ink junkie, a paper fiend and a word addict ... I'm cracked out on poetry and my Woman hate to see me go down this road, setting me up for intervention... Friends and Family saying put down the poetry, We Love You and We Want You Back, it Hurts Us To See You Like This... You're Killing Yourself but You're a Poet that don't Know it...got me over here Pissed off, like how dare y'all tear my eyes up and corner me with hugs ... Got me accepting help and packing my bags, off to a place where they can help me break this
Habit....
So this is my farewell ,... I'm off to rehab ... Closing the door on my
Amy
Whine House
before I Kurt go Bang!!!.... I got too much ink in my veins .... Just promise me you won't forget my name as I ink stain on your soul... The wailing

99 ATTRIBUTES

Women will be the only ones at the crucifixion ... My Cry was Voiced and Somebody Listened,.. And I Leave my Scriptures for y'all to ponder and Revisit ....
Sssshhhh Goodbye My Beloved Friends...
I'm here now... But little do they know...
I snuck in my Pen..

"I have written only one poem from different angles..."

El-Shabazz

99 ATTRIBUTES

*A Special Thanks
To Sister Kim Morrow,
Who Believed in me
from The Start.
I can't
Thank you enough for
Your Faith & Dedication!!!*

*Your Brother,
El-Shabazz*

99 ATTRIBUTES

www.ingramcontent.com/pod-product-compliance
Lightning Source LLC
LaVergne TN
LVHW051058080426
835508LV00019B/1950